Title

How to Increase Sales and Double your Income

Proven Methods to Generate Consistent Sales Leads

By: Adele Toral

Copyright

ISBN: 978-0-9969532-1-4   (eBook)

ISBN: 978-0-9969532-0-7   (paperback)

#

Table of Contents

About the Author

Adele Toral is a Business Consultant with 18 years experience in Sales and Business Management. She went up the ranks from a copier Sales Representative to a Director of Sales in Telecommunications. She has helped restructure many companies from various industries with her strategic methods. She has the ability to improve a company's bottom line quickly by passing along her proven techniques. Her focus is on relationship selling, customer retention and repeat business.

Introduction

Sales—you may ask yourself what makes me so special that I'm writing a book about it. I do have a story to tell, one that might inspire you to hang in there if you are just starting out in sales and struggling or if you have many sales years under your belt and are burned out and jaded. The ideas presented here may point you in the right direction and give you hope. There is a silver lining at the end of this madness, and in this book, I will give you tips that will show you how to get there.

When I was growing up, I wanted to be many things, all of which would leave a mark in the world. My eight-year-old self wanted to design houses and buildings and have a city under her name! While girls that age are thinking of dolls and dresses, I was thinking of how I was going to do great things and stand out in the world. In my mind, I went from one career path to the next, with me being a great success in all of them. By the time I was fourteen, I had decided it was time to get a job, but the fact that I was a full-time student and not eligible for working papers didn't stop me. I started canvassing after school (pretty much knocking on doors) to see who would hire me, an underage girl, for an after school job. I found a clothing factory (to put it nicely, this was more like a sweatshop) that was willing to hire me. So, every day after school I would go to this "factory" and sew. I was working with immigrants and ladies four times my age. When I received my first paycheck and saw that I had earned all that money, I realized that financial freedom was very important to me. I learned with this experience that whatever I decided to do in life, I needed to want it enough to sacrifice any instant gratification. With this new awareness, I decided that I was the sole creator of my destiny. An entrepreneur was born!

As years passed, real life got in the way of my dreams; I settled in a traditional role, got married young, had a daughter, and put aside my dreams of conquering the world. I had a well-paying nine-to-five job and felt secure in all aspects of my life. However, when I least expected, my life took a turn.

After having pretty much what I considered job security for many years, I was laid off. I was given a nice severance package, but nevertheless, I was unemployed . . . yikes! What was I to do next? I was newly divorced, was forced to fend alone for my daughter and myself, and was given a deadline to move out of the apartment I was renting. I had no savings, my credit went bad, I had no child support, and obviously, I had no job. Instead of panicking, I remembered that little girl who was not scared of anything and had big dreams, who thought that everything she could imagine she could create. I said to myself, *I can do this . . . I got this!*

The first thing I did was put all my goals in writing. I went to Staples and got the largest sized poster board I could find. I wrote all the things I wanted and added pictures from magazines to reflect these goals. I included things such as the apartment we would live in, the

location, the size, the school my daughter would attend, even the Minnie Mouse sheets she

would have on her bed. I then pinned the poster to a wall where I would see it several times a

day. I focused on these goals, and I thought about them all the time.

Did I get all the things I asked? You bet ya! This story began eighteen years ago, I'm still

in sales, and I'm still creating my destiny. I am now ready to share with you, aspiring

salesperson, or someone who would like to be successful in any aspect of their career. I will

show you the methods I used and continued to use to increase sales and pile up those

commissions. Keep reading; I will list my techniques for success and overcoming adversities in

this wonderful world of sales!

Disclaimer

Although the author has made every effort to ensure that the information in this book was correct at press time, the author does not assume and hereby disclaim any liability to any party for any loss, damage, or disruption caused by errors or omissions, whether such errors or omissions result from negligence, accident, or any other cause.

This book is not intended as a substitute for the medical advice of physicians. The reader should regularly consult a physician in matters relating to his/her health and particularly with respect to any symptoms that may require diagnosis or medical attention.

While every effort has been made to give an accurate representation of how to maximize your sales, there is no guarantee that you will earn any money. Any product that tells you otherwise is misleading. Even though this industry is one of the few in which incredible earnings potential can be realized, there is never any guarantee. Examples in this book are not to be interpreted as a promise or guarantee of earnings. Earnings potential is entirely dependent on the person utilizing the training programs, strategies, tools and resources.

How to Use this Book

I suggest you follow certain steps to get the most of out this book.

Read the entire book, not stopping to note or highlight anything.

✓ Once you read the entire book, go back and start highlighting the points that you'd like to focus on the most or that you need some improvement.

✓ Make sure to do all the practice exercises. If you have a paper book you can fill out the answers directly on the book or on a separate piece of paper if you have an eBook.

✓ Once you have come up with your goals and listed them, make sure to read them and think about them at least three times a day.

✓ When you think of your goals, get passionate about it. If you can go to a mirror and look at yourself in the eyes and tell yourself, "I can do this"!

✓ Once you highlighted the points that you are more interested in, at least once a month go back and re-read them. Unfortunately, this is not a one-time fix. This is something you need to do for the rest of your working life. As humans, we get very comfortable and eventually forget what it was that made us successful and the steps we took. Because of this, its imperative we continue learning what we already learned.

If you like the techniques in this book, I am available for coaching and online training. For a free consultation go to my website: http://toralconsult.com or email info@toralconsult.com

Chapter 1: The First Priority in Sales: You!

"Choose a job you love, and you will never have to work a day in your life."

-- Confucius

The title of this chapter may not make sense to you if you are in sales. We are always told in selling that the customer is always right, to listen more and talk less, and to always talk in terms of the other person. I will say these statements are certainly true but only to a certain extent. We spend so much time thinking about what the prospect wants to buy and how we can sell it, that we forget about the most important person: YOU. When starting a career in sales, you must invest in yourself, including every aspect of your life: physical, mental, and emotional. A balanced life translates to more sales.

Let's begin with "sleep." Did you know that the number one reason salespeople do not do well in meetings is because of lack of sleep? Not sleeping enough impairs your thoughts, your responses, and your reactions. You may think you are fine and alert; however, what you don't realize is that you are operating on autopilot. When you don't sleep enough (and don't get me started on those of you who fire up on caffeine all day; that can be even worse than not sleeping enough)! Your mind can easily wander from thought to thought, and you are not paying as much attention to what the other person is saying. You may miss a point or an objection that can make or break a sale. In medical studies, it was found that people who sleep less than six hours or over eight hours a day had a shorter lifespan of about a decade compared to those who slept around the seven-hour mark. So oversleeping can be just as detrimental to your body as under sleeping. Studies have pointed out that sleep is more important than food. Let's say you don't eat anything for a week. You'd probably be hungry, weak, and thinner. But you'd be fine as long as you have water. Now let's say you deprive yourself of sleep for a week. You wouldn't feel so good. You would slur your words; you wouldn't be able to stand or do anything. So why is sleep one of the first things we're willing to sacrifice as the demands in our lives keep rising? The reason is that we continue to live by a myth: Sleeping one hour less will give us one more hour of productivity. Not getting enough sleep hurts our health, our concentration, and our mood.

Here are some tips to help you get better sleep:

- Stick to a sleep schedule. Try to go to sleep at the same time every night and wake up at the same time every day.

- Don't go to bed hungry or too full.

- Create a bedtime ritual. This could be taking a warm bath or reading a book before bed.

This will trigger sleep since the body will see the ritual as a sign that is time to sleep.

- Find a guided meditation track for sleeping. You can find these on any phone app store or iTunes. I like to use "Calm" from the Apple app store

The bottom line is that its imperative that you get deep, relaxed sleep so you can function properly and be alert all day.

Another aspect of us that is neglected is the childlike desire to learn and grow as a person. Most people spend their school years learning new things, reading, and exploring. Then they grow up; either they start climbing the corporate ladder, or they get married and start to raise and support a family. With such a hectic schedule, who has time to pick up a book, let alone refresh their skills and take a course or go to a seminar? It is very important to keep your skills "fresh," especially in this era of technological advancements. Everything is obsolete as quickly as or faster than the time it took to develop. Work on yourself. If there's one advice you can take from this book, it is to keep a childlike curiosity for life and never stop learning new things.

When I started in telecommunications, I was hired as an outside sales person. Every day I would show up in the morning and print a list of companies, about a hundred each time, and then head to a Barnes & Nobles, which became my home away from home—I practically lived there! Back then, there were no eBooks or much information online to research. I would sit at their café, and with my cell phone, I would crank out about one hundred calls until my ear was burning from the heat of the phone. After I had made the calls, most of my day was free, so I

would grab a few books and read, read, read, taking notes of all the important points I read. I still

have those notes going back to 2003. Many of the ideas and concepts I use are from those books

I read. I was obsessed and willing to do what it took to succeed in this field, even if it meant

camping out in Barnes & Nobles every day!

Desire, perseverance, willingness to sacrifice, relentlessness, and tenacity are the traits

that successful sales people and athletes have. To succeed in any aspect of your life, you need to

put all your focus on what you want to achieve. You can't just go halfway; you are either

mediocre or you are a winner. Which side of the fence do you want to be?

Many people have the impression that if you're successful, especially in sales, it was just

luck, or things were handed to you on a silver platter. It is very hard for the average person to

understand that you make your own luck. You do this not only by working hard but also by

working smart. You may think the phrase "knowledge is power" is a cliché, but it isn't. The

more you know, the more luck you have. Your prospects want someone who's more

knowledgeable than they are, someone able to provide them with information and guidance so

they can make an educated decision. And who's better than you to provide them this

information? Most people don't have the time or the inclination to do research. And that's where

you come into play. You will be the trusted consultant who will do all the research for them. You

are the one that will give the prospect the information he or she needs to make an educated

decision. Being an expert in your field equates to "trust" in the prospect's mind. To be on top of your game, you need to put in the extra effort, meaning that you always have to know the latest industry trends, current events, and news. For example, I always start my day by reading different periodicals, such as Google News (free on the web). It has the latest information available, and it's updated throughout the day. I always go straight to the business and technology sections, and if I find an article that's interesting and resonates with a particular prospect or customer, I forward it. Doing such things shows you are thinking of them and have taken the time to listen and know what may be of interest to them.

You may be thinking; I don't want to study; I don't want to spend hours a day learning new things. I already went to school; I've been there and done that. My goal here is to motivate you to learn again in a way that you will enjoy and want to do it. There are different ways to learn. Some people learn from reading, some learn by writing their thoughts on paper, and some learn by doing (I assume you like to read since you got this book). I learn using all three methods! Let me give you an example of how I learn by doing: On my first sales job at Minolta Business Systems, I used to make a lot of introductory appointments with people that weren't really in the market to buy my products. I was criticized for doing this. People would say that it was a waste of time, that it would slow down their sales, and so on. I had a reason for doing this, and it greatly paid off. Not only did I learn what people's thoughts were about my product, but I also learned how to be a great presenter, and I learned about the competition from the strengths and weakness of the prospect's current products. I had nothing to lose by going to these meetings and so much knowledge to gain. Because I was not expecting much out of this, it made me more confident in what I was selling. And by constantly going over my products and services, I learned the information quicker and became more persuasive in selling it. One strange thing started happening as well; I was turning these so called "not looking to buy anything people" into very interested "tell me more about your product" prospects! I then realized that I didn't only want to go after the people that were in the market to buy, but I also wanted to go out there and create a need! And when I did this, I had very little competition, if any, because prospects were not looking to buy in the first place.

Here are some tips for personal growth:

• Dedicate one hour of your most productive time of your day to the most important person in the world. Yourself! Learn yoga or meditation, do something that puts your mind in tune with your body and your senses.

• READ books! Choose some that provide you with motivation and personal leadership.

• Give yourself permission to fail, and when you fail, seek out the lesson learned and grow from the experience.

• Be an expert in your field. Learn your product or service specifications inside out. Take courses.

Most importantly, learn something new every day. But even more importantly, learn the same things over and over again! There are a few ways to motivate yourself to always be learning. Whatever the task is, no matter how boring, consider all the good things that will come once it's finished—the status, commissions, and job security you will get from being the top in your field.

Create deadlines by which tasks have to be completed or schedule fixed activity blocks. I often schedule appointments with myself. If I time the project I need to accomplish, I feel more compelled and motivated to finish it on time without interruptions.

Create habits; automate your behavior. I love philosophy, and one of the philosophers I most admire is Aristotle. His train of thought was that anything can be mastered through habits.

How do you use the drive to succeed to motivate yourself? Some people are motivated to do the things that can make them successful while others are motivated to avoid the things that can make them fail. While each of those people has a different motivation style, the drive to succeed is still the common thing between them all. Understanding your motivation style is the first step you should take to motivate yourself. Let's suppose that you found that the desire to become successful is the thing that motivates you the most. In such a case, you can use visualization to motivate yourself. Visualization will ignite your drive to succeed because it will help you realize how great it will feel when you reach your goals. If you discovered that you are motivated to avoid failure instead of achieving success (this is what motivates me), then all you need to do is use fear to motivate yourself. You can visualize the bad things that might happen if you don't work hard or if you don't take a certain action, and thus ignite your drive to succeed. Using both positive and negative motivation together can have a very powerful impact on your desire to succeed. For example, you can visualize the good things that will happen if you succeed and then visualize the bad things that might happen if you fail.

Exercise: Chapter 1

"It's not about ideas. It's about making ideas happen." —Scott Belsky

LIFESTYLE BALANCE PIE WORKSHEET

On a blank piece of paper, draw a large circle to represent your life.

Thinking of your life as a pie, divide it into slices and then label each piece with an area of your life that is important to you. (e.g., Family, friends, spirituality, romance, health, work, recreation,

personal growth, money, physical surroundings, etc.)

Within each slice, draw another line as a ruler. Think of the pie's outer edge as being completely satisfied (10) and the center as being totally dissatisfied (0). Give a rating to your level of satisfaction in each of the areas you've listed by placing a dot to indicate the degree of satisfaction you have in each particular area of your life.

After completing the rating for each slice, connect the dots to create a new outside perimeter of your pie. What does it look like? Is it round and full, and ready to put on the table for everyone to see? Or does it look like there have been bites taken out of it? Think of it as being the tires on your car. What would the ride be like? Would it roll along smoothly and effortlessly? Or would it be rough and bumpy?

Then ask yourself (and answer) the following questions:

- Am I living a balanced life?
- Are my real values and priorities reflected here?
- Am I involved in too many activities? Is there too much on my plate?
- How much of my day is spent caring for others? For myself?
- Are there areas of my life that need more of my attention?
- Is there a dream or desire that keeps getting put off that I'd like to focus on?
- What area(s) needs more attention? Where is less attention needed?
- What changes do I want to make? What can I do to "round out" my life?

To move forward to a more balanced lifestyle, take steps to providing more time for and start filling in the areas with gaps—those spots where it looks like a piece of your pie is missing — because it is! When doing so, be sure to place your focus on the complete picture of your life, not just particular areas. After all, it's the big picture that "living a balanced life" is all about. [1]

Work Life Balance

With so many of us torn between juggling heavy workloads, managing relationships, and family responsibilities, and squeezing in outside interests, it's no surprise that more than one in four Americans describe themselves as "super stressed." And that's not balanced—or healthy. In our rush to "get it all done" at the office and at home, it's easy to forget that as our stress levels spike, our productivity plummets. Stress can zap our concentration, make us irritable or depressed, and harm our personal and professional relationships.

Over time, stress also weakens our immune systems and makes us susceptible to a variety of ailments from colds to backaches to heart disease. The newest research shows that chronic stress can double our risk of having a heart attack. That statistic alone is enough to raise your blood pressure! While we all need a certain amount of stress to spur us on and help us perform at our best, the key to managing stress lies in that one magic word: balance. Not only is achieving a healthy work/life balance an attainable goal but workers and businesses alike see the rewards. When workers are balanced and happy, they are more productive, take fewer sick days, and are more likely to stay in their jobs.

Here are a few practical steps we can all take to loosen the grip that stress has on us and win back the balance in our lives. Read on and reap the benefits.

At Work

Set manageable goals each day. Being able to meet priorities helps us feel a sense of accomplishment and control. The latest research shows that the more control we have over our work, the less stressed we get. So be realistic about workloads and deadlines. Make a "to do" list, and take care of important tasks first and eliminate unessential ones. Ask for help when necessary.

Be efficient with your time at work. When we procrastinate, the task often grows in our minds until it seems insurmountable. So when you face a big project at work or home, start by dividing it into smaller tasks. Complete the first one before moving on to the next. Give yourself small rewards upon each completion, whether it's a five-minute break or a walk to the coffee shop. If you feel overwhelmed by routines that seem unnecessary, tell your boss. The less time you spend doing busy work or procrastinating, the more time you can spend productively, or with friends or family.

Tune in. Listen to your favorite music at work to foster concentration, reduce stress and anxiety, and stimulate creativity. Studies dating back more than 30 years show the benefits of music in everyday life, including lowered blood pressure. Be sure to wear headphones on the job, and then pump up the volume—and your productivity.

Give yourself a break. No one's perfect! Allow yourself to be human and just do the best you can.

At Home

- The same technology that makes it so easy for workers to do their jobs flexibly can also burn us out if we use them 24/7. By all means, make yourself available—especially if you've earned the right to "flex" your hours—but recognize the need for personal time, too.

- Divide and conquer. Make certain responsibilities at home are evenly distributed and clearly outlined—you'll avoid confusion and problems later.

- Don't over commit. Do you feel stressed when you just glance at your calendar? If you're over-scheduled with activities, learn to say," no." Shed the superman/superwoman urge!

- Get support. Chatting with friends and family can be crucial to your success at home—or at work—and can even improve your health. People with stronger support systems have more aggressive immune responses to illnesses than those who lack such support.

Stay active. Aside from its well-known physical benefits, regular exercise reduces stress, depression and anxiety, and enables people to cope better with adversity, according to researchers. It'll also boost your immune system and keep you out of the doctor's office. Make time in your schedule for the gym or to take a walk during lunch—and have some fun!

Treat your body right. Being in good shape physically increases your tolerance to stress and reduces sick days. Eat right, exercise and get adequate rest. Don't rely on drugs, alcohol or cigarettes to cope with stress; they'll only lead to more problems. Get help if you need it. Don't let stress stand in the way of your health and happiness. If you are persistently overwhelmed, it may be time to seek help from a mental health professional. Asking for help is not a sign of weakness—taking care of yourself is a sign of strength.[1]

Chapter 2: The Advantage of in Person Cold Calling

The trick is in what one emphasizes. We either make ourselves miserable, or we make ourselves strong. The amount of work is the same. – Carlos Castaneda

There are many ways to generate leads these days, especially with technology and social media. But nothing can replace face-to-face meetings.

As I mentioned at the beginning of this book, after suddenly being unemployed, I had no idea what I would do that would give me enough income to support my daughter and myself. The jobs that were available for my credentials were not enough to pay for a place to live, let alone raise a child, so I needed to get creative. Since I had a positive mind frame and I was focusing on my goals poster, I had faith that everything would work out. I still had a gym membership, so to decompress and not go crazy, every morning I would head to the gym before going out on interviews. One day a young man started a conversation with me, and he told me he had a brand-new house, a luxury car all paid off, and he traveled often . . . I was impressed. It seemed to me he had it all under control financially. I asked how he was able to have all these things at only twenty-eight. He answered, saying, "I'm in sales!" So I started asking him all

kinds of questions . . . I wanted in on this. I asked what kind of sales it was and what kind of

degree was needed. He explained that to make it in sales, it wasn't so much the college degree

that you had or even the experience. It was about the sales skills and the people you knew. He

said he would help me go to interviews and would coach me on how to get into sales. I didn't get

a job with his help, but I did get the information that I needed to get started in this field. I started

looking in the sales section of The New York Times and applying to every job that I found

interesting. One that called my attention was for Minolta Business Systems; it was for a copier

outside sales position. I sent them my resume, and I was called in for an interview. On this

interview, I was given a pen and asked to sell that pen. I think I did a pretty good job selling the

pen because the woman had me talk to somebody else in the company. After I had left the

interview, I felt confident I would get a callback. But after a few days when I didn't hear back, I

knew I needed to fight for this job. I didn't realize back then how important follow-up was to

sales. I left a couple of messages to the person that interviewed me, but did not receive a

response. I decided to call back the second person who interviewed me and left her a couple of

voicemails as well. Eventually, I did get a callback. And later on, after being hired, I was told

that the manager went to the person who interviewed me and told her, "Can't you see that this

person has what it takes to sell? You have to call her to come in and work for us!" So my

persistence worked, and it's still working to this day.

I will say that this copier job was the best thing that happened to my sales career. I always

heard that if you can sell copiers, you can sell anything else, and better than others! I should say that copier sales have the most competition and the most rejection rate out there. You either get

stronger from it, or you end up leaving sales altogether. I decided to get stronger and fight; losing

was not an option for me. I truly owe the success I've had in sales so far to the time I spent as a

copier rep. On my first day on the job, I was told that I was given a starter territory, which I later

found out was a territory no rep had been successful in selling. It encompassed the area around

14th Street at Union Square in New York City from river to river. After only a one-week training

session, I was handed a pack of copier paper in different colors, and I was told to pick a color

and make hundreds of flyers. I was also directed toward the "Coles Book" (Cole Directory). This

is a sort of phone book that lists companies with some contact information. (It's still available at

the NY Business Library.) My manager said either you're knocking on doors, or you're cranking

the phones, and that was pretty much the job description. One of their rules was no reps at the

office from 10:00 a.m. to 3:00 p.m. I went a step ahead, and I left at 9:30 a.m. and got back at

4:45 p.m. Only when I was on the phone would I stay a few hours more on some mornings to

make calls. On my first day out on the field, I headed to The Port Authority building. The good

thing back than, is that there were no issues getting into buildings; there was no high security as

there is now. That building is huge, and it was very scary when I saw so many metal doors that

were all offices on each deserted floor. If there's one thing that I've learned in my life, it is to feel

the fear and do it anyway. I learned to go after what I want without overthinking things. So I

knocked on every door, handing out flyers and saying the little bit I knew about the product I was

selling until eventually a company said, "We're looking for a copier!" I made an appointment,

came back the next day with my manager, and made my first deal, with a $500 commission. I

was so excited knowing all I had to do was knock on these doors, and this would translate into

lots of money! I said to myself, "Wow, I'm going to knock on one hundred doors every day!"
And I did! On my second month, my commissions were $5,000! This was 1998, the value of that
amount is about double or more now.

In-person calling gives you access to clues that you would never have a chance to
uncover over the phone. How the prospect's business looks is a major indicator of the type of
person they are. In-person calls will help you gather as much information as possible since
people are more willing to talk than if you call them on the phone. You get a chance to see the
company with your own eyes, physically interact with individuals, and get a sense of how the
organization functions. Being able to see the prospect's business is one of the main reasons why
in-person calls are so effective. When you walk into a business, you have the chance to talk to
the receptionist at the front desk; you can get an idea of the size of the company, what equipment
they are using, etc. By seeing things in person, it lets you know if a follow-up is worth your time.
It also gives you the ammunition you will need to set an appointment with the person in charge
of purchasing what you are selling.

You should have these three goals in mind when meeting a new prospect:

√ **Meeting the Decision Maker.** The decision maker is not necessarily the owner of the
company; it's someone that has the power to accept or decline your offering. This can be
an office manager, an IT manager, or a controller.

✓ **Gathering Information**. While you are at these in-person calls, make sure to collect all their contact information: phone, email, etc. Find out what providers they are using for their services or products, and ask what the current size of their company is. Yes, you can research this online, but things may have changed from what's available to the public. This information will give you an idea where your services match theirs.

✓ If you are not able to meet with the decision maker, find out if you can set up an appointment with them at a later date.

On your next in-person call, keep these key points in mind:

• Never underestimate the receptionist. They can be your biggest ally by getting you in or your worst enemy by blocking you out.

• When speaking to the person at reception, be polite and personable. Use their first name.

• Treat the receptionist with respect. Start off the conversation on a casual, positive note

• Be aware of your surroundings. Anything can be an important clue that will help you move the sales cycle forward.

Sales can be difficult. You need to give yourself challenges to keep growing. Focus on accomplishing something you haven't yet. Remind yourself of past successes. When you are feeling down, remember the time you procured that big meeting or closed a very difficult sale.

- Avoid negativity and negative people. Avoid whiners and complainers at all cost. Negativity attracts negativity.

- Hang out with winners, feed off their energy. It's the best thing you can do for your career and life.

- Take negative vocabulary out of your life. Avoid saying the word hate or similar words. Replace any negative words or thoughts with the positive equivalent.

In-person calling can be fun (I love meeting new people and prefer it to making calls on the phone). Your success in meeting potential buyers in person will not be so much dependent on your expertise and knowledge as on your attitude. A sincere, positive attitude goes a long way toward getting people to trust you. Salespeople have to deal with more negativity than almost any other profession. For every deal signed, there's bound to be countless unanswered calls and emails that fall through. Instead of focusing on the negative, remember that salespeople have better chances for income growth. You have the opportunity to change what the dollar amount will be on your next paycheck; you are not just working for a set salary. Remind yourself of the positive aspects of selling and being able to make things happen for you. Every time I get down on my job (I'm human, and there were times when I wanted to give up on sales), I always remind myself that this is the most incredible field to be. You have the freedom to make your destiny; you are not tied up to a salary that can take years to increase.

Start seeing your sales job as having your own business. Think of the desk you sit on and phone you use as a rental. This mindset alone will increase your sales. You wouldn't be looking at the clock counting the minutes until five o'clock to leave your own business. You would have the energy and drive to keep pushing yourself. In sales, as with your own business, you have the ability to decide that this month, quarter, or year you will make X amount of money, and that's a beautiful thing! Focus, set your goals, and persevere; things will happen!

Exercise: Chapter 2

"Failing to plan, is planning to fail"

PREPARING YOUR PRESENTATION

Preparation is key to the success of your presentation. Even some very experienced presenters come unstuck when they decide to "wing it".

However, preparation is much more than just deciding what you are going to say. A whole range of variables need to be prepared for as part of the preparation stage.

In order to prepare, we should always think about answering these questions:

WHY?

Why are you giving this presentation? What is your agenda and what are you hoping to achieve from it?

It could be to sell a product or service either internally or externally, or it could be to introduce a new idea or concept to an organization. It may be an update in company procedures or imparting knowledge as part of a training program.

WHAT?

What is my objective? What do I want the outcome to be? Although fairly closely linked to the "why" stage, it is important to be clear in your mind what the SMART (Specific, Measurable, Achievable, Realistic and Time Bound) objectives actually are. Do you want them to buy something from you? In which case, how much and in what period of time? Answering these questions will help to give you the focus for your presentation and should be the overall driving force behind your talk.

WHO?

When making a presentation to your audience it is important to understand who they are and what their objectives and needs are from the presentation. It is highly likely that whatever the subject area, you will be directly or indirectly selling something to your audience. Basic sales principles teach us that before you can sell, you must establish a need. By the time you come to make your presentation this need should be completely established, as this is your opportunity to sell whatever message it is that you want to get across.

Some questions you may wish to ask yourself about the audience are:

- What is their level of knowledge or authority?

- Why are they there and what do they expect?

- What do they want to know?

- Are they internal or external?

- Are they there voluntarily?

- How many people will be there?

WHEN?

Decide when in the day is going to be best in order to get your message across. The best time to give a presentation is first thing in the morning. At this time, people are fresher, have had less time to think about other issues and are much more likely to concentrate.

Always give prior notice together with any preparation that you wish the audience to make.[2]

When someone listens to you:

7% of meaning is in the words you speak.

38% of meaning is in your inflection.

55% of meaning is in your facial expressions.

and body language.[3]

Chapter 3: The NEW Way to Dial for Dollars

"You have to be burning with an idea, or a problem, or a wrong that you want to right. If you're not passionate enough from the start, you'll never stick it out."

— **Steve Jobs**

Let's talk about the scariest instrument a salesperson will encounter—the phone! Don't let this small device intimidate you. You CAN conquer this scary monster as long as you have defined goals before using it. You need to make the phone your friend because you will be using it often, but not exactly for the purpose you may think.

Just the thought of calling people you don't know and trying to sell to them brings a shiver to most sales peoples' spine. There should be a very distinct purpose of why you call on potential customers. I do not believe in selling a product or services over the phone on an initial call.

The only reason for calling potential buyers is one of the following:

- Procuring an appointment.

- Getting their email to send information.

- Going over a proposal and answering questions.

- Following up.

Before making calls, you should write a script but never use it. Sound strange? Let me explain why. The fastest way to get shut down on a call is to sound like a machine saying something that was obviously memorized. The script should be only a guideline to remind you of the points you want to cover on your call.

Before making calls you want to do the following:

✓ Summarize what you are offering in a sentence or two.

✓ Know a couple of benefits of what you are providing.

✓ List a few companies that are using your services (preferably in their industry or area close by).

If you get the attention of the person you are speaking with, proceed by saying that you will be in their building visiting another company and that you can "pass by" for a few minutes to introduce yourself and explain more of your offering. "Close" the call by saying, "Is it okay for me to pass by on Tuesday around 2 p.m.? It will only take a few minutes." It is very important that you make it clear that it will be only a few minutes. The perception the prospect should have, is that you will be in the area meeting someone else. You don't want them to feel any pressure about meeting you; this is the only time during the sales process that you don't want to make the potential buyer feel special. You must make it very clear that you will be in their area and not making a trip just to meet them. People don't have time to meet with every salesperson that calls them, so their first reaction is to say, "No, we're not interested," or "We are all set." If they sense you are looking for a formal meeting, you will probably lose them, and they'll say they are not interested. Remember that when you call on potential buyers, they are usually not looking to buy your product or service; you also catch them off guard. They don't want to waste your time, and they especially don't want to waste their time! BUT if you make this all about just introducing yourself and giving them information so they can file it for future reference, it's an easier pill for them to swallow. The gist should be that you want the prospect to know you and about your product or service, so they can call you in case that something comes up. If you follow these guidelines, your appointment-closing ratio will go up to 90 percent! Once you meet with the prospect, if you have a compelling story to tell, many of these "intros" or "pass by" meetings (as I like to call them) will end up turning into formal meetings. Most of these meetings will take place standing at the reception area since you made it clear on the call this was an informal introduction. However, if you have an interesting story to tell, eight out of ten times the potential buyer will invite you into their conference room, and you will have a formal meeting without asking for one! My strategy is always to get the prospect to move the process forward themselves without realizing that I am the one orchestrating every step. You need to make them feel that they are the ones in charge and making every decision along the way.

When making calls, there're a few things you need to keep in mind. Preparation should be your number one priority. Having all the information readily available about the companies that you're planning to call will do wonders. Being prepared will give you confidence and ease any nerves you may have about making calls. Having a script that you read a few times before calling but never follow as written is helpful. You never want to sound like you are using a script; you need to be as natural as possible, almost like this call was the only call you made that day. Keeping the conversation very general and very casual will give you a better chance of landing a meeting or at least getting an email so you can send them information.

The following are some key points to remember:

- Ask for what you want. It's the reason you are calling.

- Ask great questions if the potential buyer shows an interest.

- Be confident in yourself and what you are selling.

- Be honest—it is the best approach.

The second reason to use the phone is to get a decision maker's email so you can send information. Emails are VERY important. They are as important as getting that introductory meeting. Use emails as a tool for strategic follow-ups, negotiating, and closing deals. The third reason to use the phones is to set a meeting or conference call to go over a proposal you already have sent them. A meeting or conference call to go over a proposal is very important because it will give you a chance to smoke out any objections. Ask tactical questions to help you learn if they are a serious contender and what their decision-making process and the time frame is.

Let's talk about voicemails. Many salespeople avoid voicemails. They either don't leave messages or leave very long commercial-like recordings. Most of those long-winded messages will never be heard. Use voicemail very sparingly. The shorter the voicemail (ten to fifteen-seconds) the more likely you will get a callback. After sending an important email, you can leave a voicemail letting the person know about the email you sent earlier. Combining the two mediums is an effective way to move a sale cycle forward. Remember, voicemails should be concise; leave any long explanations for when you get the prospect on the phone. You only have about five or six-seconds before a person stops listening and hangs up, so you better have your message within that time frame.

When making calls, DON'T do any of these:

- Apologize for calling; this shows a lack confidence.

- Eat when making calls.

- Get distracted by text messages, emails, colleagues, etc.

- Guess answers to questions. If you do not know the answer to a question, promise to find out and call them back.

- Have your cell phone off when you are prospecting. You will be tempted to look to see who is calling or texting.

- Over script the calls.

- Pitch something you don't understand.

- Promise anything you cannot deliver.

- Slam the phone down.

- Sound bored and uninterested.

- Repeatedly call the same person that's not responding; you are likely to get blocked.

- Use industry jargon too much. Use simple, easy-to-understand language as much as possible.

- Use unnecessary humor.

- Talk too much. Be concise!

- Worry about failure.

- Make calls when you are unprepared—not researching who you are calling first and not having answers to common objections.

Don't force your prospect to meet you. If they don't want to meet, ask one more time in a different way. If they still say no, ask to email the information, get their email, and call it a day.

The fourth and most important use of the phone is follow up. If I were to describe sales as a whole, I would say I work in the "follow-up business." Good salespeople spend most of their time following up. And those that don't do enough follow-up are mediocre at best. Unlike fine wine, follow-ups don't get better with age. So it's important you follow up promptly.

There are many methods to follow up:

✓ Change your medium of following up often. For example, don't always call them on the phone to "check in." This will be a turnoff, and they will stop picking up, or worse block you.

✓ Alternate emailing, calling at off times to leave voicemails, and sending a letter (no one sends letters anymore; you will stand out)!)!The point is keeping them guessing how they will hear from you.

✓ If you are in sales, you need to have a LinkedIn account. Request your prospects and leave motivational quotes or articles on your feed to keep yourself and your brand fresh in the prospect's mind.

✓ Keep track of current events, and when you bump into an article that may interest a prospect or customer, send it to them.

Realize that prospects have a timeline and budgets to consider before moving forward with a decision, so patience is a necessity to keep a good relationship going until they are ready to buy. They may also need more information to make sure they are making the right decision about your offering. Go through the process. Don't go after instant gratification, but instead look at this as a long-term process.

Make sure to provide prospects something of value each time you follow up with them. It could be a special offer or incentive to get them to make a decision now. It could be customer testimonials that demonstrate the value of your business. With each follow-up, show them ways in which they can benefit from working with you. Use reminders from Outlook or a phone app that prompt you to follow up. Don't rely on your memory to make these calls. Focus on helping, providing information, and building a relationship. Do this without expecting a sale right away, and your intentions will show through to the prospect.

When people trust and have confidence in you, they will be more inclined to buy from you. Even if they don't buy now, if you keep a good relationship, when it's time to buy, they will remember to call you. You need to be creative in your follow-up process. After your initial call, follow up with an email with different information than what you discussed on your call. Never give all the information you have at once. Space it out during the sales process; this will bring more focus to each topic and keep the interactions and relationship growing.

Follow-ups are not just for prospects. You need to follow up with current customers as well, to avoid churn and get repeat business. After you make a sale, check in with the customers immediately after delivery to make sure everything went smoothly. If problems arise, make sure to resolve the issue as soon as possible. This will gain you even more trust and will provide you with more repeat business. Also, good customer service will provide you with word-of-mouth referrals that can generate new clients for you. Remember major holidays. These are good times to send holiday cards or emails to keep you in their mind. I especially like holiday cards since they may leave it lying around and see it when they are ready to buy. You should treat customers just as you would treat a friend. You wouldn't spend months not checking in with your friends, would you? Keep in touch, send an article you think will interest them. Doing such things will go a long way in keeping customer loyalty and repeat business for years to come.

The final factor to think about when following up is that this will not be a one-step process. Some of the largest accounts I have opened had taken several years of follow-up before I closed them. If you do this as a process without overthinking things, you will grow your business continuously and eventually double or more your income.

Exercise: Chapter 3

"Not following up with your prospects is the same as filling up your bathtub without first putting the stopper in the drain." — Michelle Moore

Define a Marketing plan. Fill in the lines below your plan.

Checklist

Describe your market and the characteristics and size of each market segment; review key market trends

1)

2)

3)

4)

Compare the distribution channels for reaching customers (e.g., direct sales or through retailers).

1)

2)

3)

4)

Profile your competitors and what they're offering.

1)

2)

3)

4)

Review the effectiveness of previous marketing initiatives such as advertising campaigns or seasonal sales.

1)

2)

3)

4)

Assess the profitability and sales potential of different customers and market segments, and of different products or activities.

1)

2)

3)

4)

Decide who to target among both existing and potential customers; decide which products to push and those which need updating or replacing.

1)

2)

3)

4)

Set specific objectives: for example, retaining existing customers, increasing order sizes, selling new products or winning new customers.

1)

2)

3)

4)

Decide how you will price each product or service. (example if you will be sending and email campaign or making your 50 calls plan ahead of time if you will be offering a discounted offer)

1)

2)

3)

4)

Plan how you will promote your products or services, and how you will keep in touch with customers.

1)

2)

3)

4)

Identify customers' purchasing cycles to timetable marketing activities.

1)

2)

3)

4)

Confirm the implications of your marketing plan for the rest of your business: production and training requirements, for instance[4].

1)

2)

3)

4)

Chapter 4: How to Use Email Effectively

Your income is directly related to your philosophy, NOT the economy. – Jim Rohn

When I first started working telecommunications and technology sales, I didn't know how to compose a professional email. My mind would go blank, and I never knew how many pleasantries were too many or not enough. I reread everything I wrote out loud before sending out the message (I probably looked crazy to others as I was mumbling), and I made sure to have a conversational tone when writing. As I progressed in my email venture, I noticed that certain keywords or something as simple as a bolded sentence would provide swift replies, often with the information I needed to move a sale forward.

I also learned I had less room for error by writing short emails. I was concise in my writing, and I managed to get my point across succinctly. If there's one thing you should learn in this chapter is that "less" is often "more." So take your time to write a few short sentences when sending out emails. If you have trouble condensing your message, one of the methods I use is bullet points. Using lists lets you cover all your points with concise sentences.

Not only did I realize that with short emails I was saving time, but my reply rate more than doubled as I uncovered these techniques. The more responses you have with valuable information, the faster your deals will close. At the end of your emails make sure to request some action from the person you are writing to, whether it is asking for a reply with specific feedback or asking closing questions so you can find out the validity of the lead you are working with.

Keep in mind that I hadn't read any books or had any guidelines as to how to write effective emails; I learned everything from trial and error. I find that failing gracefully and learning from mistakes is the only way to grow in sales. If you expect this journey to be smooth without lots of failures in between, then this may not be the career for you. The more successful you become in sales the higher the number of failures you will have. They say that superstar baseball players strike out 70% of the time. The reason they are superstars is because they play the numbers, they hit the ball more times. Play your numbers right and you will succeed, guaranteed.

As I got better at writing emails I started seeing the results; people were replying back with the action I requested from them, and they felt compelled to give me what I was asking for. I was on a mission to perfect this art that I found to be so useful and time-saving for selling. I find that email is my first go-to for cultivating relationships and providing superb customer service. Let's say you conduct your business mostly on the phone; not only prospecting but following up and doing some customer service along the way. If you spend an average of 20 to

30 minutes talking on the phone per person, how many people do you think you will talk to in a day? You will also need to do other tasks such as writing proposals, attending meetings, handling conference calls and maybe doing some admin work, so you wouldn't be able to reach as many people, right? When it comes to email, you can reach hundreds or more people a week than you could ever reach by using the phone. However, be careful about sending cookie-cutter emails that are spam. I send very strategic personalized emails even if I am using a template. The best way to turn somebody off and have them put you directly in their junk mail is to send an email that is obviously an advertisement for your service or product with no catering to their particular needs. Email is one of the most important tool you can use to double your earnings and take you to the next level as long as it's done strategically.

Some things to keep in mind before sending out emails:

There is a lot of time spent sending out emails, without a lot of data or analysis on how effective those emails are. You need to keep track of the type of messages that are getting are getting the most responses. Keep track of what time of the day you are sending them and even what day of the week they go out. Keeping track of this can help you fine-tune your efforts.

When it comes to marketing emails, while most people consider the workweek to be the most active time to send them, research has found that more work-related emails are opened over the weekend. Also, the longer the email subject line, the less likely an email is to be opened. I spend more time thinking of catchy subject lines than working on the actual body of the email! If the email looks like spam or a time waster, people will not be compelled to open it.

Email secrets that will pay off:

1) Make sure your first line attracts attention. People's attention span is very short; you need to say something that will catch their interest quickly.

2) Keep your emails brief and easy to read! Nothing will turn your prospect off more than long, information-packed emails. Break up your sentences into paragraphs to make them easy to read and more accessible.

3) Ask for a return response. Always thank them in advance for their consideration.

4) Say on your email that you will follow up by phone if they don't respond. 8 out of 10 will respond ASAP! Say that you want to make sure they received the email and that if you don't hear from them you'll follow up with a call. This increases your response rate, since they usually don't want to take the call.

The secret to the success of any follow-up system is in scheduling the additional follow-ups and then following through.

Don't expect that just sending out a bunch of emails is going to generate leads. For emails to work there must be a strategy and a plan in place. Sending mass emails requires a very organized system to make sure you are targeting the audience that's interested in your message, and that you are not over-emailing to those that don't want to hear it for a while. Remember, use short sentences and paragraphs. Make it easy for people to read and understand.

Make sure you make it clear as to what the email is about. Construct the email with a single topic. Use bullet points to explain a point, and if you have more than one high point to go over then say you will send a separate email with the rest of the information. The best way to get someone not to read your message is by sending a long, scary email. They will save it to tackle it at a later time, and they may never get back to it.

The Secrets to Successful Email Marketing

The single most important activity you will have in your sales career that will guarantee your success is database management. I have kept a database that I created in 2003, in which I have about 13,000 companies and thousands of email lists. I laboriously assembled my database by compiling the information I obtained from meetings, cold calls and referrals. So when I send emails out they are not spam; I am sending emails to people I have interacted with in one way or another at least once. The fastest way to get shut down and blocked is by sending unsolicited emails to people who have never heard of you. Choosing the right frequency for sending emails is critical and something many salespeople neglect to plan.

Email marketers will naturally want to send more emails if they're working well, but the risk is always there that they'll reach a tipping point where some subscribers will have had enough. I personally only send marketing emails once a month. I send each and every email conscientiously, noting in my data base what type of response I received after sending it, and saving those that showed lack of interest for the following month. I have been following this process for nine years with excellent results.

Here are ten steps to successful email marketing:

- Consolidate Your Names

- Build Your List of Email Addresses

- Develop Your Email Campaign Mix

- Write Your Emails

- Choose Your Recipients

- Send Your Email Blast

- Process Opt-Outs

- Process Bounced Emails

- Follow-Up Step

- Refine and Repeat

Recognize Your Audience

Understanding the audience and knowing how they would like to view an email is important. Tailor the subject line, content and layout of an email to target the segment that is trying to be reached.

Content

Be conversational with the message and substance of an email. People want to connect with people and not with automated messages that are naturally sent out in bulk. The high response rates of personalized messages are proof that being personable works. Provide information on goods or services, free giveaways or rewards to give it value while appealing to the target audience.

Measure Success and Results

Always measure the success of an email campaign and the results. It is important to keep track of the number of emails delivered, opened and the kind of responses received. Keep track of this information so you can better evaluate and adjust your email campaigns. By modifying and retesting campaigns, eventually you will get it right, and this doesn't mean you won't have to change your message because this will always be a work in progress.

The number one reason recipients unsubscribe from your emails is that you're sending too many emails! The top reason people opt out of email marketing is usually because they receive too many emails. Part of the inbound methodology of email is not only sending the right message but also not sending the same message repeatedly. You need to set up appropriate intervals depending on the market you are trying to reach.

I consider email to be the most important medium to run my business. I recommend you make this yours too and that you take the time to analyze and master sending emails. I have put together some guidelines, but the best way to find out what works with your customers and prospects is to try it yourself and to be diligent in learning how to do it correctly.

Exercise: Chapter 4

"In the midst of chaos, there is also opportunity"

— Sun Tzu

When you start your email campaign, you are taking a Marketing role. You need to ask yourself some questions before sending out an email campaign.

The 10 Questions Marketing Should Ask Sales

1) Who is the primary customer type?

2) What can you tell me about this primary customer? (e.g., position, age range, educational background, management style, industry experience, information sources, trade shows attended, etc.

3) What are the customer's required conscious needs? (i.e., what do they say they want)?

4) What are the customer's required unconscious needs? (i.e., what do they really want)?

5) Who are the key influencers within and outside the customer's organization that impact the buying decision?

6) What is the customer's typical buying process and how long does it take?

7) What do we do differently or better than anyone else from our customer's perspective? What do our customers say makes us unique?

8) What do our top competitors do differently or better than us? What makes them unique?

9) What are some of your best stories about when different customers were thrilled with our product or service?

10) What are the top 3 deliverables I can provide you to make your job easier, more fun, or more successful?

Who is Your Buyer Persona?

A "buyer persona" is a semi-fictional representation of your ideal customer — the real buyers who influence or make decisions about the products, services or solutions you market. The buyer persona sits at the nexus between sales and marketing. Defining or redefining the buyer persona is a high-leverage activity that takes the strengths and insights of both marketing and sales. It allows them to come together, focus on what's most important, drop what isn't, and then get busy driving sales and building the brand.[5]

Chapter 5: Trial and Error. Failing Your Way to success

Sometimes when you innovate, you make mistakes. It is best to admit them quickly and get on with improving your other innovations. – Steve Jobs

There's controversy out there about learning with trial and error. People say that its time-consuming, and it can be discouraging. Thomas Edison didn't feel this way; he just couldn't get it right. After about ten thousand experiments, he couldn't get a new type of battery to work. But Edison didn't see it that way, and instead he saw it as "now I know ten thousand ways that the battery won't work!" He did get it to work after thousands or more experiments, but he never gave up, no matter how many times he failed. People have this misconception that if you are bound to do great things it should be easy and you are just born with this unusual gene that makes everything happen. The reality is that it's nothing like that. This is a quote from Edison, and it's exactly the method I use to come up with new ideas: "When I want to discover something, I begin by reading up on everything that has been done along that line in the past — that's what all those books in the library are for. I see what has been accomplished at great labor and expense in the past. I gather data of many thousands of experiments as a starting point, and then I make thousands more." [6]

Errors teach us new things about ourselves and our environment; you will never grow if you don't make mistakes. Through trial and error, we learn what works, and what doesn't. It's a reality check. When we experience the results of slip-ups, we get a message about which of our efforts are working and which are not. Other areas of our lives change for the better. One way to gain the greatest benefits from our mistakes is to ask ourselves questions such as "What made me chose to do what I did?" "Was it my idea, or did someone suggest this?" "Did I fail for lack of effort or giving up too soon?" "Did I do my best to make this work?" And so on.

Being in sales and always carrying a monthly quota, I didn't have time to wait months or even weeks to find out if things were working or not. I needed to see results or at least improvements toward the right direction for me to continue doing whatever it was I was doing. I use the trial and error method. Looking back at my life, I now realize that I've always used this method, even when I didn't know I was using it. It's how I found my first job when I was an underage teenager and how I landed my first sales job and started a life long career. My methodology is "if it's not working, quit quickly before it's too late." Too late for me means not hitting that monthly goal.

You may sometimes feel as if no matter what you do, things don't seem to work, and no matter what you try fails. You may be down in the dumps and a little depressed if you are not hitting your numbers. In this case, it can be your attitude that's blocking things for you to be successful. So you should use the most promising solution you have in front of you at that moment and give it a chance. Just make sure to be consistent for a period to see if you get results. For example, let's say you decide you will do all it takes to make three initial appointments a week following the methods I gave you in this book. Don't just do this for a week or two and say, "Oh well, this didn't work for me." Give yourself a period of, let's say, sixty or ninety days, keep doing what you are doing, and just add this as a side project. For example, set a goal of having an average of twelve introductory appointments a month. Keep track of these meetings, either inputting the information in a database or Excel spreadsheet. Do the follow-up techniques suggested in this book and see what results you get. Perhaps on month two you close one or two of the people you met in week one when you first got started, and on month three you are maybe closing three or four of the accumulation of leads you are finding. Understand that this is a process; perhaps you can't hit the numbers I just referenced, and maybe that's because you don't have much experience, and you are just starting out in sales. Don't get discouraged; the darker it is the closer you may be to that brilliant rainbow. But even if you are closing one deal a month after month two, that's one more than what you had before you did this project. And think what is going to happen in year two and even year three if you keep this up! That's what happened to me when I was first struggling; no one saw it coming until one day I exploded and became #1, and I've never looked back since then.

In sales, you need to have a survival instinct, and you need to be on the prowl and ready when an opportunity presents itself. You will be surprised how subtly opportunities show up and how they can slip by and go with the competition if you are not paying attention. To make sure that you are at the right place at the right time, you need to expand and diversify what you are doing. Get your eggs in multiple baskets, and this way if one of the basket's eggs goes bad you always have another basket to fall on.

Now, all this talk of trial and error won't work if you don't learn from your mistakes and don't move a step forward each time you err. The secret of learning from trial and error is that you recognize that you made a mistake. If you start blaming others, or your boss, or the company or the universe, you detach yourself from any lesson, you could learn from the experience. However, if you face the situation head on and admit that you are responsible for the mistakes you've made and that there's only yourself to blame, the opportunity for learning and growing are there for you. Wise people admit to their errors and even welcome them, since they know they are a step closer to making it, just like Thomas Edison did!

Here is a list of the benefits you can receive by making mistakes:

✓   It lets you know how much further you are from where you started.

✓   You learn what matters and what does not.

✓   It teaches you something new that you didn't know.

✓   You may discover an option you never considered.

✓   You may find a warning that can prevent bigger future mistakes.

✓   It will put ego aside and make you humbler.

✓   It will increase your knowledge.

✓   You learn what works and what doesn't work.

Here's a quote that resonates with my life: "I think we all wish we could erase some dark times in our lives. But all of life's experiences, bad and good, make you who you are. Erasing any of life's experiences would be a great mistake." - Luis Miguel.

Looking back at the hardships I had to endure in my life, I am grateful to have lived them. I'm now able to take those experiences and help other people by telling my stories and giving them shortcuts so perhaps they will not suffer as much as I did. In the past, I didn't have the resources and means to get the help that I needed to fast track my career. Any experiences, good or bad, make you what you are today so don't be afraid of mistakes or avoid them. Welcome the good and the bad the same way, and know they will only make you stronger and wiser. "Mistakes are the portals of discovery," James Joyce once said. How else will you discover the many possibilities out there if you don't make mistakes? The way I see it, if I meet someone with a big ego that doesn't admit their mistakes and blames everyone under the sun, I know that person's days are numbered. They won't get very far in life, and things will be temporary. They will jump from one place to the next because their ego will not let them advance. I've seen this happen too many times throughout the years. It's the law of life, so be humble, accepting and kind and good things will come your way.

Let's say you followed the advice in this chapter, you used a trial and error method, you admitted any mistakes, you analyzed the cause of your error, you asked yourself the questions needed to uncover the cause of your mistakes, and now what? Cut your losses and move on! That's it, don't dwell on it for days, weeks or months. There's nothing more that will bog you down than having a pity party about how you messed up, and how nothing goes well for you. No, that is not what this chapter is about. You get up, brush off the dust and start your next trial, and if you fail, you get up again and keep doing this until you make it!

The bottom line is that if you analyze everything you do and don't do and just go about your day in a robotic manner not paying much attention to your surroundings, you will get a step further every day to reaching your goals. Keep that fighting spirit inside of you. What movies motivate you? I especially enjoy movies like *Braveheart, Gladiator and 300*. What these movies have in common is that the protagonist had to overcome unbearable circumstances and, instead of giving up, they gave all they had with passion and, foremost, with shrewd creativity. These characters (*300* being from a historical event) found a way in circumstances that most would walk away from. They persevered until their goals were achieved.

What motivates you? What fires you up? Is it sports? What biographies of your favorite athletes have inspired you? Guess what famous athlete said this: "I've missed more than 9,000 shots in my career. I've lost almost 300 games. Twenty-six times, I've been trusted to take the game-winning shot and missed. I've failed over and over and over again in my life. And that is why I succeed." Michael Jordan. If this doesn't inspire you, I don't know what will! Here's another from him: "I can accept failure. Everyone fails at something. But I can't accept not trying (no hard work)."

If Michael Jordan, the greatest basketball player of all time, admits to making the most mistakes as compared to any other player, that only brings us to one conclusion: If you are not making mistakes you are not heading to the road of success. You should embrace mistakes instead of fearing them. When you get on the phone tomorrow, you can ask yourself "how many mistakes will I make today?" Remember that the more mistakes you make the closer you are to becoming a Thomas Edison or Michael Jordan. Everything and anything is possible; you don't know where life will take you tomorrow. But you sure can control what you do today and gear the direction of your life to where you want it to go. Just know that nothing in life is impossible and that impossibility is what your mind knows to be impossible. You have the power to change your mind, to change your circumstances and to change your luck! Take it from a person who was unemployed, raising a child without a penny to her name, and I managed to do well for myself and have continue to do so by never being complacent, always admitting my mistakes, being kind to everyone and remaining humble in my demeanor.

Exercise: Chapter 5

"The best way to predict your future is to create it"

— Peter F. Drucker

Willpower and Self Discipline Exercises

Exercise no. 1

You are sitting in a bus or train and an old man or woman or a pregnant lady walks in. Stand up and give up your seat, even if you prefer to stay seated. Act so, not just because it is polite, but because you are doing something that you are reluctant to do. This is an exercise in overcoming the resistance of your body, mind and feelings.

Exercise no. 2

There are dishes in the sink that need washing, and you postpone washing them for later. Get up and wash them now. Do not let laziness control you. When you know that in this way, you are actually strengthening yourself, it becomes easier to take immediate action, despite laziness and the desire to procrastinate.

Exercise no. 3

You come home from work and sit in front of the TV, because you feel too lazy and too tired to take a shower first. Do not succumb to the desire to sit in front of the T.V, and take a shower immediately.

Exercise no. 4

Do you like your coffee with sugar? If you do, then for one whole week drink it without sugar. Do you drink three cups of coffee each day? If you do, then drink only two cups a day for one whole week. Such exercises prove to you that you can control or change your habits, and this inner strength.

Exercise no. 5

Do you, like many others, like to read some unimportant gossip in the newspaper or magazine? Then, for one whole week, abstain from doing so. This might not be easy, but its good for your training. I am not telling you to do so indefinitely, but for only one week.

Exercise no. 6

If you have the choice of going up with the elevator or climbing the stairs, choose climbing the stairs. However, climb the stairs only if it's not a high story, and you are in good physical condition.[7]

Chapter 6: What Would Aristotle Do? The Power of Habits

"Keep away from people who try to belittle your ambitions. Small people always do that, but the really great make you feel that you, too, can become great."

-- Mark Twain

In my countless hours at Barnes & Noble, I will never forget the discoveries I made of authors and philosophers and how they left a mark in my life. One philosopher who still echoes in my heart is Aristotle. I have always been intrigued with the why, when or who of philosophy. I tend to think in a very structured way, so I felt very excited when I found a philosopher who I believed in and who taught things the way I'm used to learning. I realized that his methods were the ones that I would use to turn my life around. His theory was simple and easy to grasp. His fundamental belief was "habits." It still baffles me how habits can make or break one's life.

One of my favorite quotes from Aristotle is: "We are what we repeatedly do. Excellence, then, is not an act, but a habit."

Let me explain what this quote means to me. When I first read it, I realized that, to be extraordinary, you didn't have to be born a certain way, come from certain parents or have a certain education. I learned that by changing the things I did and by forming good habits it would help me achieve the goals I wanted to achieve.

For example, Mozart was a pianist and a great one. By Aristotle's logic, the reason that Mozart was a great musician was because he repetitively practiced playing the piano until he became magnificent. If you want to achieve anything in your life you have to practice things until you master them; there's no way around it. Habits and repetition are what make the greats great. Name any successful athlete or artist and read about their life and you will find that each and every one of them repeatedly practiced their craft over and over again.

Now, mind you, you don't need to be perfect from day one. Let's say that you want to improve making calls and setting up introductory appointments. Maybe you feel that you're terrible on the phone, or you can't get past the receptionist, or if you do, you get the phone slammed down at you. So you're asking yourself what you should do next, how can you master making these calls and setting up the meetings? The answer is simple: keep doing it consistently until it suddenly happens. There's no secret formula or potion that you drink that will make you better instantaneously. You just need to just "do it."

Beware of questionable theories you find on the Internet as well as on some training classes. They say things like "Cold calling is dead" and "Get leads while sleeping." If it sounds too good to be true, it is. Good salespeople make six figures, and it's not by doing nothing. Any books out there that promise a glorious career by not doing the hard things necessary to succeed are lying. They are just trying to find ways to sell more books by selling a dream. The business of sales is hard, especially at the beginning. You need to work hard, you need to want this badly and be hungry; there are no shortcuts once you choose this career. But once you make it, you will find that it was all worth it, and that the rewards will surpass the pains.

If you haven't seen the movie *Boiler Room* I advise you to rent it or buy it. It's a "must watch" for any aspiring salesperson. In this film, Ben Affleck has a bunch of rookies in a group interview. He's very abrupt in his speech, and he's very concise as to what he expects. He starts several sentences with "Act as if …" I can't say the rest because what follows won't go with the sentiment of this book and some of you might blush! But you will get the point when you see the movie. If you are not confident yet, "Act as if you are the top producer of your company" and "Act as if the prospects need you, and they will buy from you." People know and can feel what you are thinking of yourself without you saying a word, so make sure you are only thinking positive thoughts at all times.

Let's say you want to give it a shot and get started and try some of the things I've mentioned in this book. You wish to form a good habit, and you will begin by setting three appointments a week. Stop reading now and go to the practice chapter for this exercise. Mark your calendar for 60 days from now and write down the goals that you are going to achieve in this timeframe. Write that you will make 12 appointments a month, preferably three a week, and from these appointments you will close at least one deal in the second month. After you have this in writing and saved, put together a script. Then get a recorder—most smartphones have a recording apps—and record yourself saying the script over and over. Don't say it exactly as you wrote it; just say the most important points in a conversational tone. Every time you record yourself and you find mistakes, stop and start over. Keep doing this, recording, listening and recording again. Once you feel natural and comfortable with the recording, then get some of your family and friends to call you so you can practice on them.

You may find that, even though you felt confident with the recordings, you might feel nervous speaking to somebody else, even if it's a friend. You might feel that you are back to square one and sound a bit nervous. Don't despair, just keep calling your friends (that's why I asked you to call several in case one gets tired you call the next person). Once you feel comfortable making the calls with your friends, then start making the real calls to potential buyers. You will probably not sound excellent and you will be very nervous but that's okay … "act as if." At least now you know your script, and if you were able to be natural and confident with your friends, you know that eventually you will be calmer while making the real calls.

The next step is to make a goal of the number of calls you will make to set these meetings. Let's say that you decide to make 50 calls a day until you achieve your three-meetings goal. In the beginning, you might end up making the 50 calls every day and only getting one meeting for the week. But if you continue being consistent with the calls, your closing ratio will get better to the point that you might only need one day of calling to set three meetings. In my case, if I can reach ten decision-makers on the phone my ratio is that I will close three for a meeting. That's a great closing ratio and if I can do this so can you; it only requires discipline and determination.

When I started in sales, the only advantage I had was that I created habits. I did the same things over and over every single day without a break. The worst thing that you can do is go on a marathon one day and make 100 calls and then not make any calls for a week because then you're not practicing and you're not improving. Making it a habit of doing the calls daily, for example, will get you where you want to be. Slow and steady wins the race, so remember this.

"Excellence is an art won by training and habituation. We do not act rightly because we have virtue or excellence, but we rather have those because we have acted rightly. We are what we repeatedly do. Excellence, then, is not an act but a habit." Aristotle, (384 BC - 322 BC) Greek Philosopher

When I started in technology sales, there weren't as many choices out there as far as online training or even getting information on the Internet as there are now. When I decided to start training on routers and networks, the only choice available was to head to a local college and sign up for a course. I had to go to a CCNA class that trains engineers to take a very complicated, long test to get this certification. I do not regret taking these courses since they helped me immensely to increase my sales, but going to these classes after work and staying until 10 o'clock and then reading and studying the big books was a lot to handle. These days there's no excuse because you don't even need to leave your house due to the vast number of online courses available today.

You're no longer in a 9-to-5 job or going to school full-time, where you had set hours. The minute you start a sales job you signed up to having your own business, and what do people that have their own business do? They work, and they work very hard. Especially if they're starting out with a new company, they don't have set hours or set days because they're fighting to make their business succeed. You need this mindset to make it in sales.

If you want to double your income one year from now, make sure you go to the exercise chapters and follow the instructions. Then make a promise to yourself that you will follow the advice in this book. Make a commitment to creating good habits, such as starting to train more and controlling how you spend your time. Then write down what your income will look like the following year and I guarantee you, if you have the perseverance and hunger to follow the steps in this book, there's no question in my mind that you will double your income. Feel free to go to my website and tell me all about it at http://toralconsult.com. I would love to hear from you and give you some more tips as well.

Here are some habits that you can start implementing right away:

- Get up at least one hour early every day. Use this time for reading or watching some educational YouTube videos as you drink your morning coffee. In the morning, your mind will be more open to new ideas and concepts since you will have rested the night before.

- The second thing is to visualize what you plan to do for the day. Sit down comfortably, close your eyes and see yourself having a successful day. See yourself going into the office or, if you work at home, sitting at your computer and making the calls you plan to make and setting the appointments you plan to set and even closing the deals you're looking forward to closing!

Another habit that you should get into if you aren't already doing it is reading every day. There's no better way to exercise the mind than by reading. With the plethora of e-books today you can read from your phone anywhere. Read on the train if you take mass transit or while waiting in offices for an appointment, at the doctor's office; no matter where you are you can get your phone out and read a book or put in your headphones and listen to an inspirational audiobook. If you drive long distance, most books are now in audio so that's another way to get information that you wouldn't be able to get otherwise.

If you find that you spend too much time on social media throughout the day, turn off all the notifications and make it a habit to check your social media and personal emails only twice a day. Social media is great for keeping in touch with family and friends and for businesses to keep new information in front of their customers. But it can also be very destructive if you don't control how much you use it.

One more area you need to monitor is your texting. I know many people who are addicted to their phones and feel they need to answer every text within a millisecond after they receive a message. The way I have my notifications set up is that I have all company emails going to a folder and all my customer and prospect emails going into another. I set my notifications to receive them from the customer and prospect folder only. Anything else can wait and does not need an answer in an instant. If it's an emergency people can call you.

Exercise: Chapter 6

"Failure is simply the opportunity to begin again, this time more intelligently." –

Henry Ford

Find new perspectives that no one else has taken (or no one else has publicized)! Leonardo da Vinci believed that, to gain knowledge about the form of a problem, you begin by learning how to restructure it in many different ways. He felt that the first way he looked at a problem was too biased. Often, the problem itself is reconstructed and becomes a new one.

Visualize

When Einstein thought through a problem, he always found it necessary to formulate his subject in as many different ways as possible, including using diagrams. He visualized solutions, and believed that words and numbers as such did not play a significant role in his thinking process.

Produce

A distinguishing characteristic of genius is productivity.

Thomas Edison held 1,093 patents. He guaranteed productivity by giving himself and his assistants idea quotas. In a study of 2,036 scientists throughout history, Dean Keith Simonton of the University of California at Davis found that the most respected scientists produced not only great works, but also many "bad" ones. They weren't afraid to fail, or to produce mediocre in order to arrive at excellence.

Make novel combinations

○ Combine, and recombine, ideas, images, and thoughts into different combinations no matter how incongruent or unusual.

○ The Austrian monk Grego Mendel combined mathematics and biology

○ To create a new science of heredity. The modern science of genetics is based upon his model.

○ Form relationships.

○   Make connections between dissimilar subjects.

Da Vinci forced a relationship between the sound of a bell and a stone hitting water. This enabled him to make the connection that sound travels in waves. Samuel Morse invented relay stations for telegraphic signals when observing relay stations for horses.

Think in opposites

Physicist Niels Bohr believed that if you held opposites together, then you suspend your thought, and your mind moves to a new level. His ability to imagine light as both a particle and a wave led to his conception of the principle of complementarity. Suspending thought (logic) may allow your mind to create a new form.

Think metaphorically

Aristotle considered metaphor a sign of genius, and believed that the individual who had the capacity to perceive resemblances between two separate areas of existence and link them together was a person of special gifts.

Prepare yourself for chance

Whenever we attempt to do something and fail, we end up doing something else. That is the first principle of creative accident. Failure can be productive only if we do not focus on it as an unproductive result. Instead: analyze the process, its components, and how you can change them, to arrive at other results. Do not ask the question "Why have I failed?", but rather "What have I done?"

Have patience

Paul Cézanne (1839 – 1906) is recognized as one of the 19th century's greatest painters, and is often called the father of modern art, an avant garde bridge between the impressionists and the cubists. During his life he only had a few exhibitions though his influence on subsequent artists was great as an innovator with shape and form. His genius, however, was not evident until late in life. He was refused admission to the Ecole des Beaux-Arts at age 22 and his first solo exhibition was at age 56. His genius was the product of many years' practice and experimental innovation.[8]

Chapter 7: Time Management Techniques for Winners

"There are no secrets to success: don't waste time looking for them. Success is the result of perfection, hard work, learning from failure, loyalty to those for whom you work, and persistence."

— Colin Powell

Time management is the ability to control what you do when you do it and how long you do it.

Throughout this book, I have mentioned aspects of sales that are very important to implement for you to succeed. For these steps to take place, you need to find a way to incorporate the different tasks throughout your day. The only way to be able to get enough sleep, make the calls, go to meetings and even spend time with your friends and family is if you learn to manage your time wisely. If you are unable to manage your time, you will not be able to take care of yourself and do all the different ideas presented in this book.

I chose to go with the time management topic further into the book because I wanted you to learn a few of the things that have made me successful first and then show you how to incorporate these ideas throughout your days, weeks and even years later on. There are so many different ways that you can manage your time; there are apps, computer programs, alarms, everything under the sun to help you manage your time. The point is that you have to find a technique that works for you and you have to stick to it to be able to do the different things needed to be successful. The worst thing you can do for your career is to procrastinate and not take action about managing your time. You have to find a way to push yourself not to let this happen. In this book, I will include a chapter to give you guidelines as to how to start managing your time. But even if you write down the things that you need to do and when you need to do them, you still need some reminders and alarms that will prompt you to get things done. I like to remind myself of tasks, so I use all sorts of gadgets and alarms to push me to the next level and make me do my work.

Let's begin by going over following up. I went over in a previous chapter the importance of following up after a meeting or when you send out an email, etc. When you start making your daily calls, not everyone is going to be able to meet with you. Many of the decision makers you get on the phone will ask for you to send them information via email, that will require you to follow up. Or they will ask you to call back the next month. These follow-up tasks will add up to the point that they will be overwhelming, and without a system to remind you to do these tasks, you will surely be in a big mess and not knowing how you even got there. Let's start with Outlook, as most people in business use it. Outlook has a calendar with the ability to set alarms.

Some people like using Outlook to remind them of calling, and you can certainly give that a try. I don't like using it for calls, because if I have too many follow-up tasks in one day, I need to either leave a bunch of windows open in my task bar or if I close them I might forget. My primary use for Outlook calendar is to set up conference calls. I like that I can invite multiple people, and on the notes of the invite I add the conference bridge information. So Outlook is my conference call alarm.

Being that most of the products I use are Apple, one of the apps I like using is the reminder app that is on the iPhone, iPad and all the Apple computers and even watches. I like to use this app for the smaller tasks, such as such as making calls for a follow-up. I like that it syncs with all my devices so when it's time to make a call, no matter which device I'm using, I will get that reminder. If I'm not ready to make the call at that moment, I can snooze the call for an hour or even into the next day (just be careful not to choose "complete" because it will disappear from your pending reminders, and you might forget). I also manage a very robust database that I've had for thirteen years at the writing of this book; I have over twelve thousand companies with thousands of valuable contacts, email addresses, etc. When it comes to critical follow-ups such as contract date expirations, I like to add the alarm directly into my database. I may schedule calls far in advance. If I meet or speak with a prospect or customer, and I am confident that their contract is up in, let's say, eighteen months in the future; I will set an alarm on my database to remind me to call about three months before the date that they tell me their contract is due. In some cases, I'll check in even six months before because many times prospects are not sure when their contract is up. I've had situations when I follow up, and they tell me that their contract was up two months before the date they first gave me. And that they have switched to another

provider already ... now that hurts! I also like to use the Apple calendar; I use it just for meetings

or any recurring tasks. By putting the address of a meeting on the notes of the calendar, I can just

press it and use it as a map for directions, so it's very convenient when traveling to meetings.

Most of the things I use for reminders are technical. You might not be a technical person;

obviously, I'm in the technology industry, and I use all these different gadgets. But if you're not

technical, you can go to a Staples store and get a calendar book and write down all your

appointments and follow-ups on paper and just continuously look at it every day and maybe use

a highlighter as you complete the tasks. I used the paper method for many years, especially when

I started in my first sales job in 1998. No matter what you do you need to have something to

remind you to do what you need to do. You cannot count on just your memory because you will

have so many holes and unfinished projects that it will equate to many unsatisfied customers, and

your sales career will not advance. If there's one thing that I hear over and over from my clients

and even prospects is that I can be counted on. They always hear from me when they expect to,

and I always get back quickly when they email or leave me voicemails. Keep in mind that

nothing I tell you in this book will work if you don't learn to manage your time. So pick your

system to remind yourself of things as soon as possible.

Now let's talk about how you will manage your day to get everything that you need to get

done finished on time so you can have a balanced life. So you can have time to spend with your

friends and family and get your seven hours of sleep every day. Unfortunately, you won't be able

to do this if you don't thoroughly plan your day every day. I have a standard to do list that I printed out and put it on an 8 x 10 picture frame on my desk. I titled this sheet "Prioritize". I have a 10-step process of what I need to do every day and in what order. For example, my number one task is to go over my pipeline. No matter what happens, I need to work on my pipeline first thing in the morning every single day. If you spend your day working on emails, making calls, even going to meetings and you neglect the pipeline, you will fall behind, and you won't close your deals very quickly, if at all. The number one reason you are in sales is to close deals and to close them as quickly as possible, so you need to prioritize this task every single day of the year with no excuses. I have a description of every to-do item. For example, on the pipeline task it says things such as "do something to this deal every day by email or phone call or voicemail , etc." ... just a couple of lines reminding me of what to do to close a deal.

Let me tell you a story of why I came up with my daily to do list. When I started out working in the telecommunications and technology field, it was a very hard time for me. I wasn't technical at all, and I didn't understand anything about Internet access or routers or even computers ... absolutely nothing! The only thing I had going for me was that I worked hard, I had an obsession with reading, learning new things and I had good habits. All these things alone didn't help me close deals. And it didn't help me to sell because I didn't know how to talk about the products and services that I was selling, so I struggled a lot. It took me seven months to make my full quota, and the only reason I wasn't fired was because I was making big appointments with decision-makers of Fortune 500 companies. Everyone was very impressed and very curious as to how I was able to get CIOs or CFOs to listen to me and even meet with me. On my seventh month of starting in this field, I hit the jackpot when one company that I called and kept following up with finally one day they called me and said they were ready to proceed with the

order. With that one account, I made my quota. I never stopped making my quota for about a

year but then suddenly I started struggling and forgetting the things that I did that made me so

successful. My mother, who is very business-minded, gave me the advice to write down

everything that I had done in a step-by-step format and to keep it near my computer for

reference. She said if I found I was struggling I could just go back and read my notes. I decided

to condense everything in 10 steps and put it in front of me to view daily. In sales you just can't

stop learning, even if it is the same thing you already learned! The minute you feel you know it

all and you become complacent; that is the time that you will perish. Fast forward to now and it's

still the list that I am using today.

But there's more. I was finding that even though I had the list in front of me, and I knew I

had to start with the pipeline; I would get distractions such as phone calls, emails and other

things that would take over the time I had for working on my pipeline. I decided to look for

another addition to my to do list. I was able to find an app that lets me name different alarms in

the background of my computer. So when I start my day I call one alarm Pipeline, and I give it

two hours, for example, and another alarm I name Tasks and give it another two hours and a third

alarm could be Prospecting, and you could give it three hours. You can name the alarms

depending on your priorities. The good thing about this system is that if I am working on the

pipeline for 20 minutes, and I get an interruption, I stop that alarm, turn on the task alarm and

start working on whatever task presented itself. When I'm done with the task, I go back to my

pipeline alarm, turn it back on, and I'm back in business. So no matter what, I managed to get my full two hours a day of just working the pipeline. Now, you may not need all the alarms I use,

and you may be fine just using the to do list and the reminder app, for example. I have a big load

to deal with, and I need all the help that I can get to get through the day.

Exercise: Chapter 7

"The bad news is time flies. The good news is you're the pilot." -"

— Michael Altshuler

Prioritize

List 5 things you'd like to change about yourself. Example: Being able to set goals, learn to set priorities , etc.

1)

2)

3)

4)

5)

List 5 Goals (personal or career). Example to make X amount of money by X.

1)

2)

3)

4)

5)

List two of the goals you want to accomplish first. Focus on these two goals the next year.

1)

2)

Break your most important goal into four sub-goals. (If you choose to increase your sales an example is you will make 50 calls a day, you will read one a day, etc.)

Goal:

1)

2)

3)

4)

5)

Visualize Your Goals

Use the method listed in the visualization chapter and see your goal materialized several times a day. Act as if the goal is already completed.

Sample to do List

Date:	Priority*	Energy Required	Time allotted	Reward	
TASK					
Make 50 calls	5	√	2 hours	√	Coffee break

*1 = most important; 5 = least important

Chapter 8: Visualize Your Way To Success

"Logic will get you from A to Z; imagination will get you everywhere."

-- Albert Einstein

We have the power to program our subconscious minds to help us in getting what we want. Why does visualization work?

Let's divide your brain into two parts. One is conscious, and the other is the subconscious. The conscious is the adult part of your brain, and the subconscious is the child part of your brain. Children are very susceptible to their environment, and they absorb everything around them whether it's right or wrong. We always watch what we say around children, and we try not to influence them wrongly. We know that if negativity surrounds a kid he or she will not grow up to be a mentally healthy child. So we try to give the child the best environment possible. If you tell a kid they can be anything they want when they grow up, that they are doing a good job, and you always use encouraging words, the child will act accordingly. What you tell your subconscious is what it will manifest back to you. It's imperative you surround your child (subconscious mind) with positivity and encouragement to make sure you attract what you want, which is to succeed in sales. You will find that every single athlete that is at a high level first visualized precisely what they wanted their body to do. Athletes see themselves receiving the accolades, going past the finish line. Michael Jordan visualized the ball going in the basket and Michael Phelps saw his strokes in the water at the speed and precision to win a race. If you can see it in your mind first, the body will follow! That is the motto of athletes.

I've read hundreds of books on many different topics. One topic I have focused on throughout the years is the subconscious mind and how you can manipulate it to attract the things that you want. You can manifest your dreams and goals just by thinking about them all the time and programming your subconscious to accept this and go out there and find it for you. Now, this may sound easy but it's not. You would be surprised how much negativity goes through our minds just in one day. Negative interactions with others can affect us in how we think as well. When we accept what others are saying to us as true, we are programming our mind to attract this negativity, and this is the reason I stated in a previous chapter for you to stay away from negative people. You need to be very diligent and catch yourself when you have any negative thoughts and any negative words that go out through your mouth. This topic is a book in itself, and I will include a book on visualization and manifestation in one of the books in this series.

Let's focus on visualization and how you can start making changes now to double your income by next year. I will include a sheet in this book so you can write down your immediate and long-term goals with some steps as to how you'll plan to achieve this. Let's pretend you decide that your goal is to have a shiny red ball. You close your eyes, relax and count from 20 to

1 slowly as you let go of your entire body, muscle by muscle. As you do this, you visualize a

beautiful red shiny ball, the ball is in your hands you see it coming to you from the sky, and

you're so happy you have your shiny red ball. You show everybody your ball. You keep thinking

these thoughts for about 10 minutes if possible twice a day morning and night. As you visualize

your goal, one thing you shouldn't do is imagine how you will get your ball. Don't imagine going

to the store and buying a ball or having your aunt Mary bring you the ball for your birthday, none

of that! You need to wait for your mind's energy to decide the best way for you to get the ball. In

the interim, while you wait for your ball, make space in your closet for the ball, buy a rack to

keep your ball. By doing these things, you're telling your subconscious that you completely trust

and believe that you will get the ball. Your subconscious then accepts that you will get the ball,

and it will make you aware of all the situations and circumstances where you can get this ball.

Now your subconscious will be on the complete lookout for the ball, and you will see cases in

which a red ball can be found so that even if you were at the right place at the right time before

doing these visualizations you would have missed the red ball.

I used this method to get an apartment with a beautiful bedroom for my daughter and her

Minnie Mouse sheets back before I started in sales and was completely broke after my divorce. I

went further by building a wish board, which I would contemplate every time I'd pass by it.

Anything you do to get yourself thinking and visualizing what you want will do the trick. Keep

your speech positive and stay away from negativity, as those are the first steps for you to achieve

your goals.

How Visualization Works:

- It programs your subconscious to do what you want. The subconscious mind is your inner child. When you visualize what you want, you're showing your child that's it's okay to attract that thought or image.

- tap into the law of attraction. Whatever you think about most you attract. By thinking of your goals, you are attracting them to you.

- It motivates you. You feel energized, trusting you will get what you are visualizing.

- It activates your creativity. When you imagine the things you want, you learn to use the right hemisphere of your brain, which in turn raises creativity.

- Create a picture board.

I created a picture board by going to the Staples store and getting the largest poster board they had. I listed all the goals I had for the coming year. I taped pictures from magazines, and I prepared myself to move as if all my goals were already completed. I achieved each and every one of my goals! If one of your goals is to buy a car, go to the auto dealer take a picture next to the car you want and tape it to your board. If you want to travel, post pictures of where you want to go. In sales, it's imperative to want things. If, for example, your goal is to buy a new BMW with cash, you will do all it takes to make that happen if you program that in your subconscious mind by visualization.

Affirm Your Goals

To add more strength to your visualization you can also affirm your goals. Always do this in the present tense. Such as: "I have a BMW." "I make my quota every month." "I am driving my new car to work." Do you get the picture?

The subconscious mind accepts what you tell it consistently. If you tell a child, he or she is smart all the time; eventually the child will tell everyone they talk to how smart they are. If you tell the same child, they are stupid they will end up thinking and acting like they are stupid. Your mind works in the same way. Feed it good, positive thoughts and it will give you good, positive results. If you change your thoughts, you will change your "reality", and it's just that simple! Manifesting is not magic. Many people have asked me if I'm a magician and how I make things happen when other people in my same situation can't. Remember, even by complaining about small things, such as saying that you have no space to put things in and that your apartment is too small, you are telling your subconscious to keep attracting the small apartment. The mind does not differentiate when you're just venting or saying what you want. It just picks up whatever you think of the most and whatever you put the most passion and energy into when you say it or think it. Keep this in mind before you start the path of visualization.

Know What You Want

You can't possibly start visualizing when you are not sure of what you want, or if you keep changing your mind. That is why it's so important that you write down your goals first. I include a sheet in this book to write down all your goals and start a plan of action.

Decide What You Want to Visualize First

Some people don't know where to start, yet others come up with a 3-page list of all the things they want. You need to focus and pick the most critical subject first. If doubling your income and establishing your career in sales is your priority, then focus most of your visualization on that. It doesn't mean you can't visualize the guy or girl you want to marry, for example. But you can't scatter yourself all over the place where you end up not focusing in depth on any of your goals.

Believe

Let me make this as clear as possible. You can write down goals and visualize until you are blue in the face, but if you don't believe that the techniques will work, they won't. The subconscious knows what you are thinking the most strongly about. So if you are doing all the exercises but in the back of your mind you think that it's all bogus, and then your goals will not come to pass. You need to trust this system blindly, trust that things will happen. Some things you will see results right away and others, such as doubling your income, you will need to wait a year or so to see it. The point here is "act as if" until you believe that what you are asking for will happen. Have faith that the law of attraction will bring good things to your life. The more you believe, the faster things will come to you.

Focus On Your Goals Throughout the Day

If you use mass transit or have long drives to work, use the power of daydreaming. You don't always need to get yourself into a meditation trance to think about your goals. You can be looking out of a window riding a bus, and think of how happy you will feel when you can have financial freedom when you have no debts when you have savings in the bank, and you can get all the things you want and deserve. See what you want vividly, and you may find yourself smiling when thinking these thoughts randomly.

Give Your Goals Positive Energy

Always keep your thoughts positive, and fight to keep any negative feelings away from your mind, such as envy, jealousy, hate. Any of these feelings will only hinder your success. If any negative thoughts appear, politely let them go and start thinking of the positive things you have and that are coming your way.

The question in your mind should be "when" not "if" your goals will be achieved. When you do start manifesting your goals, remember to be thankful and grateful for what just happened. You need to ingrain in your subconscious that you believe in the power it has and acknowledge what the gift you just received from your inner child. This will empower your mind to continue manifesting your goals in the future.

I know this is a lot to process in one chapter, but at least it's enough to get you started into a more positive thinking environment. Make sure to do the exercises on visualization in this book. If you get started on this path, your life will do a complete 180-degree turn. You will see the results you've been waiting for all your life, and you will become a true believer! You just need to get started and take baby steps until you master this process. If it's not easy for you to sit down and do formal meditation, it's okay just to do it as you're doing your tasks throughout the day. Think of the things that you want as much as you can. I like affirmations. I like saying out loud the things I want to manifest for myself. The point is that you need to be surrounded by all the things that are positive and that you want to happen and avoid talking or thinking about everything that you don't want in your life. You shouldn't think or talk or see things that you don't want. If you don't want lack of money, stop saying that you have no money. Stop saying that your car stinks or that your apartment is too small. By consistently saying these negative things, you're attracting them into your life. Change your thoughts first, and your life will follow.

Exercise: Chapter 8

"It's fine to celebrate success but it is more important to heed the lessons of failure."

– Bill Gates

Here is a simple 10 step beginner's guide to meditation:

Sit tall

The most common and accessible position for meditation is sitting. Sit on the floor, in a chair or on a stool. If you are seated on the floor, it is often most comfortable to sit cross-legged on a cushion. Comfort is key. Now imagine a thread extending from the top of your head, pulling your back, neck and head straight up towards the ceiling in a straight line. Sit tall.

Relax your body

Close your eyes and scan your body, relaxing each body part one at a time. Begin with your toes, feet, ankles, shins and continue to move up your entire body. Don't forget to relax your shoulders, neck, eyes, face, jaw and tongue that are all common areas for us to hold tension.

Be still and silent

Now that you are sitting tall and relaxed take a moment to be still. Just sit. Be aware of your surroundings, your body, the sounds around you. Don't react or attempt to change anything. Just be aware.

Breathe

Turn your attention to your breath. Breathe silently, yet deeply. Engage your diaphragm and fill your lungs, but do not force your breath. Notice how your breath feels in your nose, throat, chest and belly as it flows in and out.

Read more: Stop & Breathe

Establish a mantra

A mantra is a sound, word or phrase that can be repeated throughout your meditation. Mantras can have spiritual, vibrational and transformative benefits, or they can simply provide a point of focus during meditation. They can be spoken aloud or silently to yourself. A simple and easy mantra for beginners is to say silently with each breath, I am breathing in, I am breathing out.

Calm your mind

As you focus on your breath or mantra, your mind will begin to calm and become present. This does not mean that thoughts will cease to arise. As thoughts come to you, simply acknowledge them, set them aside, and return your attention to your breath or mantra. Don't dwell on your thoughts. Some days your mind will be busy and filled with inner chatter, other days it will remain calm and focused. Neither is good, nor bad.

When to end your practice

There is no correct length of time to practice meditation, however when first beginning it is often easier to sit for shorter periods of time (5 to 10 minutes). As you become more comfortable with your practice, meditate longer. Set an alarm if you prefer to sit for a predetermined length of time. Another option is to decide on the number of breaths you will count before ending your practice. A mala is a helpful tool to use when counting breaths.

How to end your practice

When you are ready to end your practice, slowing bring your conscious attention back to your surroundings. Acknowledge your presence in the space around you. Gently wiggle your fingers and toes. Begin to move your hands, feet, arms and legs. Open your eyes. Move slowly and take your time getting up.

Practice often

Consistency is more important than quantity. Meditating for 5 minutes every day will reward you with far greater benefits than meditating for two hours, one day a week.

Practice everywhere

Most beginners find it easier to meditate in a quiet space at home, but as you become more comfortable, begin exploring new places to practice. Meditating outdoors in nature can be very peaceful, and taking the opportunity to meditate on the bus or in your office chair can be an excellent stress reliever.

Meditation is a simple, effective and convenient way to calm your busy mind, relax your body, become grounded and find inner peace amidst the chaos of day-to-day life. Begin meditating today and reap the rewards.[9]

Chapter 9: How to Manage your Data

The first one gets the oyster the second gets the shell. – Andrew Carnegie

Where should I start regarding having a database or CRM (Customer Relationship Manager)? It seems that every time I start a chapter I say that this is what has made me successful and who I am today. The reality is that the combination of all these different sections is what makes a successful salesperson.

I've seen it all when it comes to how salespeople manage their customer's or prospect's data. They collect business cards, have a Rolodex or plain Excel sheets lying everywhere, with lists of customer information. Sometimes I see them using Outlook to maintain their information, and it's not optimal, but it's much better than using an Excel sheet. Once the average salesperson decides to use a CRM, I find they don't actually commit to it. They don't enter the information promptly, and it is not updated enough. So when they need data quickly, they run around like a chicken without a head trying to collect information.

I've always listened to advice, especially when it came from successful people. The first thing that I did when I started at my first sales jobs in copiers was find out who the high producers were and what made them tick. I pinned it down to two people in my department. One was Eddie, who was a shrewd businessperson. Not only was he on top of his game, but he had a side gig closing deals for the rookie reps and getting a cut of their commissions. He was a closer; he closed and fast. Eddie was cool, calm and collected with his black hair slicked back. Then there was Martin, and I would say that he inspired me to do many of the things I did. Martin was the first to introduce me to visualization. He was a Buddhist, and because of what he told me I practiced Buddhism for many years and went to weekly seminars and meditation classes. This philosophy helped me with the art of living in the present moment and taught me to focus (not an easy task for me being a type A personality). Both of these individuals were making three times more money than the average salesperson at the time. There was also a third person who gave me a good piece of advice. He told me always to manage a database, that it doesn't matter what it is, but you need a place to put all your customer information in a computer and manage the data on a daily basis. I looked at him with wide eyes as if he had three heads. I was not sure what he meant. I mentioned at the beginning of this book that I started out not knowing anything about technology. But I was on a mission to find out what a database was and how I would set up one of those. I started with an Excel sheet and, after accumulating over a thousand companies, I quickly realized it was not the most productive way to handle my territory. I upgraded to Microsoft Access, and I started to get a better feel for how to manage my data. Later on, I discovered Goldmine and used it for a while, until I settled in with ACT. And it's still the database I use today. I am entirely dependent on my database; I say this as a good thing!

Here are some benefits of using a Database or CRM:

Better Customer Service

You will be able to manage your customer base with more detail. You will have all this data right in front of you. You will have access to information such as what services customers or prospects are currently using and when their contract expires all in one place. You will have their contact information of the different individuals within a company. I have it set up so that it keeps a copy of email messages inside ACT of all the Outlook emails I send out. All this information can be viewed on one page, and I can access it in seconds! I have my customers' social media pages linked to their page in my database as well. Talk about having all their information at my fingertips! Having all this data available in a matter of a click builds credibility and trust. You can help a customer in distress very quickly without having to dig for information. You will have all their records right in front of you at all times. And these files will be created by you, so you know exactly how to utilize the data you have.

Simplified Marketing/Sales

The only way you're going to send very targeted emails and keep analysis of them is by having a database to store these emails. It is the most organized way to see what messages you sent in the past and to see which ones worked and which ones did not work.

Data, data, data

What can I say? It's data, and it's important to have data for your business. As a company or a salesperson, you need to have the data for all your customers and prospects. Things such as their business size, current news, everything can be stored in detail into a robust database.

Discover New Customers

By keeping classified information in the database, you will be ahead of the game from most of your peers. Keeping good notes of every interaction with your customer and prospects will keep you organized and up to date. You will create a reputation for being someone who knows their customer and cares. Such a good reputation will in turn generate referrals, excellent references, and it will bring you new business.

Up-sell Products More Effectively

You will be able to up-sell more effectively because you will have notes and emails attached to previous conversations of needs or issues the customer might have expressed to you that you would not remember if you had not stored the information in a database.

Better Customer Retention

Because you will be able to keep all this information and history about your client, you will notice any red flags before it's too late.

More New Business

Having a database will equate to more business because you will be more organized, and you will have updated data. This will enable you to have targeted marketing for your customers and prospects.

There are various CRMs available these days. Some are very effective, but I am still stuck to ACT after all these years. The reason I like using ACT is because it is extremely customizable, and it's very focused on customer data alone. I've created companies with subcategories in groups that are not available on the average CRM out there, not even in Salesforce. It does require a lot of time and patience when you first start developing a database. Also, keep in mind that the database will never run itself; it's only as good as the information that's put into it. For you to be successful using a database, you need to be updating it every day. I find the best way is always to do it real time. Always have your database open on your computer all the time as you go about your day, and input the information as it happens. Leaving Post-it notes or business cards lying around to input later or, even worse, at the end of the week, is not going to give you good results. You will end up misplacing things or never getting around to entering the information. You can become so backed up that you will quit having and maintaining a database. Without a database your dream of doubling your income and growing from there are close to impossible, so you need to find a way to manage your information in a coordinated manner. I have closed deals with companies I met four years earlier. The reason I have been able to pull this off is because I keep detailed notes, alarms and follow-up schedules that almost always end up in me winning the deal, even if it takes a long time. Every topic in this book works as a cohesive unit. One is linked to the other and creates what a successful salesperson should be like. Below you will find out how having a database helps you with time management.

Using a Database Saves Time

Trying got get a customer record, using files and paper can be very time-consuming and unorganized. It can take several minutes of digging around to try to find a file. If things change with a customer, you may have to refill new forms to replace your file. This process is very time-consuming. With a database, everything is a click away, and you can copy and paste new contact information from an email. Promote a contact to a primary field or merge two companies together in an instant. I don't use paper at all. The only paper I use is a small pad if I need to jot down information quickly while on the phone. I have no files, no folders, no paper anywhere near my working space!

More Accessible Information

You can do a lookup with certain criteria quickly. You may want to call on IT consultants only, and with a couple of clicks you can have all the IT experts included in your database in front of you. You can create groups of companies by employee size, geographic area and much more. The possibilities are endless when you have a database in place.

Exercise: Chapter 9

"If you do build a great experience, customers tell each other about that. Word of mouth is very powerful." – Jeff Bezos

This page alone will more than cover the cost of this book. I have included a free database you can find online. Got to this link https://www.insightly.com and sign up. There are plenty of instructions and videos in the site. You should be up and running in not time.

Insightly is a great tool to help small businesses deal with the vital task of managing your contacts, organizations, partners, vendors, and suppliers. Using CRM best practices, you can see everything about a contact, from background, email history and important dates, to any projects or opportunities in which they have participated. With Insightly's web-based contact management features you won't miss a beat.

Free CRM online https://www.insightly.com Make sure to practice using this CRM throughout your day every day.

Use Insightly to manage potential business in your sales funnel. You can create opportunities to define the value of the business, manage pipelines and associated activity sets, opportunity funnel stages and categories, probability of winning, and forecast close dates.

The Insightly Calendar shows all your events and you can even display your tasks with due dates and milestones. You can also sync your Insightly calendar with Google and Outlook Calendars. When sending an email to any opportunity, you can send it through Insigthly so you can have a copy of the email within the CRM.

Activity sets: Activity sets are a way to automate repetitive tasks and events – saving you the time of creating them one by one. For example, you may want to create an activity set for your sales process – initial call, follow up email, check-in call 5 days later.

Alerts, notifications, and tasks: Insightly has a number of options to keep you on top of your busy schedule and ensure you always have the latest information. For example, maybe you want to be noticed when a task you assigned to another user has been completed, or when the details of a contact you are interested in have changed, or when another user adds new information to a project.

Chapter 10: Common Traits of Successful People

Successful people are always looking for opportunities to help others. Unsuccessful people are always asking, 'What's in it for me?'—Brian Tracy

Here are some of the traits that successful people possess. You may have some of these traits and, if you do, cultivate them. If you don't focus on them, whatever you think of the most will expand!

#1 – Results-Focused

When I started my first job in sales as a copier representative I was very observant of what everyone was doing. Everything was so new to me and I didn't know what to expect. One thing I rapidly noticed was that certain people looked like they were working very hard. They had stacks of papers on their desks, they stayed very late at the office and they were always typing "stuff" into a computer. I became very curious and wanted to find out if there was something I could learn from them. After talking to a few of these people and seeing what they were doing, I realized that they were working hard, BUT they were working on the wrong

things! Fast forward to where I am now, and all through my career I have met many people like

this (I have fallen into this trap myself many times, and snapped right out of it once I realized I

was hiding in non-results oriented work). These type of people are so scared of rejection and of

taking a risk, that they lie not only to their manager and peers but also to themselves about the

work they are doing. This type of person is very hard to catch; it's so much easier to find a

slacker that's obviously not doing anything than someone who seems focused and always busy.

What these individuals are doing is burying themselves in admin tasks. They usually have the

most organized databases, since they are meticulous entering information and making sure

everything is up to date; no job is too small for them! They will stack their Post-It notes lined up

perfectly and their desk drawers are impeccably organized. On the other hand, successful people

are always focused on "results." Everything they do is geared toward their goals. Their desks and

working environments may not be the neatest, but their results speak for itself. They get

outcomes such as closing that big deal, starting that profitable business, being the top person in

their company and so on. They do all the right steps to get to that place where they can see, smell

and even taste what they want! Don't be a paper pusher! Be like the successful people, and focus

on results.

#2 - Courageous

Successful people have the courage to do what would make others squirm by just

thinking about it. They make that dreaded call to get an appointment. They are not scared to ask the hard questions to close a deal, even if it means losing the deal altogether. Courage does not mean you will not be fearful. It just means that even though you can be scared, you have the courage to do the things you need to do in any circumstance.

#3 - High Energy

Successful people are energized. They get up early; they are the first in the office, and you can feel their energy field just by being near them. They have a twinkle in their eye and are always going places. They don't just seem busy ... they are busy, doing the right things to get them closer and closer to their goals.

#4 - Committed to Growth

Successful people are committed to growing; they are always looking for the next new thing that they can learn. They are good listeners and are very in tune with their surroundings, and they're always ready to take advantage of any learning situation. They are not judgmental of people with less education than they have. They know there's always at least one thing that they can learn from anyone.

Don't think that successful people have anything more than you as far as intelligence, beauty, or youth is concerned. Success comes from all walks of life, and the only difference between a successful person and one that's not, is hunger and the willingness to do whatever it takes to make it. If anything, these were people who were at the bottom of the barrel when they first started.

Here are some successful people that started at the bottom:

√   Starbucks CEO, Howard Schultz net worth: $2 billion. In an interview with the British tabloid Mirror, Schultz said: "Growing up, I always felt like I was living on the other side of the tracks. I knew the people, on the other hand, had more resources, more money, happier families. And for some reason, I don't know why or how, I wanted to climb over that fence and achieve something beyond what people were saying was possible. I may have a suit and tie on now but I know where I'm from, and I know what it's like." Schultz acquired his CEO position in 1987 and grew this coffee shop into 16,000 outlets worldwide.

√   The Oprah Winfrey Show, Oprah Winfrey net worth: $2.9 billion. Born in Mississippi to a very financially burdened family, Winfrey still managed to win a scholarship to Tennessee State University, becoming the first African-American TV correspondent at the age of 19. Fast forward to 1983 and Winfrey moved to Chicago to work for an AM talk show which, of course, would later be called The Oprah Winfrey Show.

√   Forever 21 Founder, Do Won Chang net worth: $5 billion. After arriving to the US from Korea in 1981, Chang actually had to work three jobs – all at the same time – to make ends meet. Eventually, he launched his first clothing store in 1984. Today, Forever 21 is a global 480-

store empire that cashes in about $3 billion in sales a year.

And the list goes on! Were these people better than you and me? Absolutely not. Make it a goal to be the best you can be.

I struggled the first months in telecommunications, I wasn't technical at the time so things were harder for me. Some people looked down at me because I wasn't selling and I didn't know anything about technology; they made me feel like a complete outcast. That situation only pushed me to fight harder to learn more and to brush off all the negativity around me. At the same time as I was going through the adversity at my job. I was raising my daughter, and she was having issues in school. I had to pull her out of school and homeschool her at night. That only gave me more ammunition to not give up. I was working a sales job, and I was a full-time teacher to my daughter as well. I've come a long way since then, but that hunger inside of me is still there. Persistence and perseverance will get you everywhere. For you to excel quickly, you need to be obsessed with whatever it is that you want to achieve. Don't worry about what others say because most people feel threatened when they see that you have potential. Some people want to be surrounded by average people, and the reason why is because if you are too successful you make them feel inadequate. They are afraid it will get out there that they're not as good as they are making it seem; so they will do all they can to jeopardize what you have. This is why it's very important to surround yourself with positive people; not doing so can hurt your chances to excel.

Let me tell you about comfort zone and the status quo. Successful people are always pushing the envelope. The more you are out of your comfort zone, the more you're growing and the better the chance of your success. You have to take your temperature every so often and see how things are. If you feel very comfortable in your job, and everything seems like a routine, stop yourself immediately! To advance, you cannot be too comfortable. If you want to challenge yourself and grow then there's always a level of discomfort, but a good discomfort. One that is filled with hope and enthusiasm of what the future has in store for you. There should never be any boredom in your life; you should have so much going on that sometimes you are not sure if you're coming or going. In order to grow you need to always be doing something new. Everything that you learned today will be obsolete very soon, so beat it to the punch and be two steps ahead of your game. If this sounds like too much, it really isn't. I live a very balanced life. I have two Siberian Huskies that I adore but they are a handful. I love doing my gardening – and it's a big garden – everyone in my neighborhood hires help while I'm planting, mulching, and weeding. I find working outdoors to be very therapeutic. I'm able to free my mind of worries, and sometimes I have the best ideas when I'm not looking for them. To do the things I enjoy, yes, I have to plan every day, and I can't leave it to chance. It's the price to pay to be able to have it all: success at work and at home as well.

Another trait successful people have is outstanding customer service. They tend to think in regard to other people. They help for the sake of helping without expecting anything back; in turn they get it all back and with interest. They understand that cultivating a relationship is most important to keeping customers and gaining repeat business.

Here a summary of the point of view of successful people:

- They are life-long learners who push themselves out of their comfort zones.

- While most people think that when they graduate college they are finished being a student, successful people remain students. They are constantly learning new things and have new experiences. They aren't afraid to try new activities and to fail at them.

- They do more than what's asked of them.

- They view their job descriptions as just the beginning of what they can do with their job.

- They are willing to fail in order to eventually succeed.

All successful people know that it doesn't come easy and they are bound to fail more than they will succeed at anything. They are willing to learn from each failure, as it will help them make better decisions that lead to success later. While many people give up after failing at something, a successful person will persevere.

Successful people:

They know that they make their own luck.

Luck is derived from hard work over time and positioning yourself for success. You won't randomly get lucky and successful people know that. They will do at least one thing every single day to put themselves in a better position to get lucky and then use that luck to grow.

They take accountability for themselves and their actions.

They aren't relying on other people to get the job done. Instead, they are looking inward and are trying to find the solutions, while leveraging their current assets. If they make a mistake, they own up to it and immediately think of ways that they can improve next time, not making the same mistake twice.

They can communicate their story effectively.

If you walk up to a successful person and ask them what they do, they will able to tell you everything in a concise manner. They know who they are, what they do and can make you believe in them. They have strong posture and are very persuasive and confident. They create instead of just consume.

While most people are busy reading emails, watching TV, or listening to a podcast, successful people are creating new tools, working on presentations, and coming up with ideas.

They are the ones who are making things that other people need instead of being on the other end

of the spectrum, consuming them.[10]

Exercise: Chapter 10

Willpower is the key to success. Successful people strive no matter what they feel by applying their will to overcome apathy, doubt or fear.—Dan Millman

To Brainstorm your goals, get a notebook and write the questions below on top of the pages. After, writing down everything that comes to mind and fill out the entire page. You should come up with a few ideas that will provide you with the "Aha" moment for each question.

Questions to ask yourself:

- What will I do to get started? i.e. Training, reading

- Who can help me and how can they help me?

- What is important to me right now?

- What are more short term goals?

- What are my long term goals?

- What are the resources I need to make this happen?

- How will I make things happen?

- What am I willing to sacrifice to make this happen?

Wrapping it All Up

Whatever the mind of man can conceive and believe, it can achieve. Thoughts are things! And powerful things at that, when mixed with definiteness of purpose, and burning desire, can be translated into riches. – Napoleon Hill

Congratulations on finishing this book! You are on the road to improving your life and doubling your income. Learning shouldn't stop here; be hungry for knowledge, keep reading and never stop growing.

Training & Sales Coaching available, for a free consultation go to my website: http:// toralconsult.com or email info@toralconsult.com

Endnotes

1. http://www.smartrecovery.org/resources/library/Tools_and_Homework/Relapse_Prevention/

lifestyle-balance-pie.pdf

2. http://www.aproposltd.com/free/presenting-workbook

3. Albert Mehrabian, Ph.D.

Professor Emeritus of Psychology, UCLA

4. http://www.marketingdonut.co.uk/marketing/marketing-strategy/your-marketing-plan/how-to-

prepare-a-marketing-plan

5. https://www.linkedin.com/pulse/20140707043247-16037464-how-to-build-your-buyer-

persona-10-questions-marketing-should-ask-sales

6. Article Source: http://EzineArticles.com/575583

7. http://www.successconsciousness.com/willpower-self-discipline.html

8. [1] http://www.studygs.net/genius2.htm

9. http://stopandbreathe.com/2011/03/04/meditation-101-a-10-step-beginners-guide/

10. http://www.forbes.com/sites/danschawbel/2013/12/17/14-things-every-successful-person-

has-in-common/

www.ingramcontent.com/pod-product-compliance
Lightning Source LLC
Chambersburg PA
CBHW032006190326
41520CB00007B/375